PRAYING Woman

365 Daily Prayers for Powerful Women

In the ancient halls of the Tabernacle at Shiloh, a woman named Hannah poured out her heart before God. Her lips moved silently, her tears flowed freely, and her spirit groaned with a desperation that only the Lord could fully comprehend. Year after year, Hannah had endured the pain of childlessness, but on this day, she approached God with renewed fervor. Her prayer was so intense that Eli, the priest, mistook her for a drunk woman. Yet Hannah persisted, laying bare her deepest desires before the Almighty.

> *"O Lord Almighty," she prayed, "if you will only look on your servant's misery and remember me, and not forget your servant but give her a son, then I will give him to the Lord for all the days of his life..."*
>
> (1 Samuel 1:11, NIV)

Hannah's earnest prayer not only resulted in the birth of Samuel, a great prophet of Israel, but it also serves as a powerful testament to the intimacy and transformative power of a woman's conversation with God.

Like Hannah, every woman has within her the capacity to forge a deep, personal relationship with her Creator through the simple yet profound act of prayer. Prayer is more than a religious duty or a list of requests; it is the heartbeat of our spiritual life, the very breath of our intimacy with God. It is in these moments of communion that we find strength, guidance, comfort, and purpose.

In today's fast-paced world, where demands on our time and attention seem endless, cultivating a consistent prayer life can be challenging. Yet, it is precisely in this busy, often chaotic environment that we need the anchoring presence of God more than ever. Daily prayer provides a sanctuary of peace amidst life's storms, a wellspring of wisdom in times of confusion, and a source of strength when our own resources are depleted.

Through prayer, we open ourselves to God's transforming work in our lives. As we bring our joys, sorrows, hopes, and fears before Him, He shapes our hearts, renews our minds, and aligns our will with His perfect plan. It is in these intimate conversations that we truly come to know God - not just as a distant deity, but as a loving Father, a faithful Friend, and a wise Counselor.

Moreover, prayer is not a one-way communication. As we speak to God, we also learn to listen for His voice. In the quiet moments of prayer, God often speaks to our hearts, providing direction, correction, and affirmation. This two-way dialogue deepens our relationship with Him and helps us navigate life's complexities with divine wisdom.

The practice of daily prayer also cultivates a spirit of gratitude and dependence on God. As we regularly acknowledge His blessings and seek His guidance, we become more aware of His constant presence and provision in our lives. This awareness fosters a deep sense of peace and contentment, regardless of our circumstances.

As women, we often juggle multiple roles and responsibilities. We may be wives, mothers, daughters, sisters, friends, professionals, or community leaders. In each of these spheres, we have the opportunity to be powerful intercessors, bringing the needs of our loved ones and our world before God's throne of grace. Through prayer, we partner with God in His redemptive work, becoming channels of His love and grace to those around us.

This devotional is designed to guide you on a 365-day journey of deepening your prayer life and, consequently, your relationship with God. Each day offers a focused theme, a relevant Scripture, and a heartfelt prayer to inspire and direct your conversations with God. As you develop a habit of prayer, may you, like Hannah, experience the transformative power of earnest prayer. May you discover the joy of walking closely with God, finding in Him the source of your strength, the object of your devotion, and the fulfillment of your deepest longings.

Welcome to *"Praying Woman:365 Daily Prayers for Powerful Women."* This prayer book is designed to be your companion throughout the year, guiding you in your spiritual journey and helping you develop a deeper, more intimate relationship with God. Here's how the book is structured and how you can make the most of it:

Structure and Themes

This devotional is organized into 52 weekly themes, carefully chosen to address the various aspects of a Christian woman's life. Each week focuses on a specific topic relevant to your spiritual growth, personal challenges, and daily experiences. From "Trusting God for the New Year" to "Cultivating a Legacy of Faith," these themes provide a comprehensive framework for your spiritual journey throughout the year.

Daily Format

Each day's entry follows a consistent format designed to guide your prayer time:

1. Theme of the Day: **A specific focus within the week's broader theme**.
2. Scripture Verse: A carefully selected Bible verse related to the day's theme.
3. Prayer: A heartfelt prayer written from a woman's perspective, addressing the day's theme.
4. Reflection Question: A thought-provoking question to help you apply the day's message to your life.

To make the most of this devotional, consider setting aside a consistent time each day for your prayer and reflection. Whether it's early morning, during a lunch break, or before bed, find a time that works best for you. Begin by reading the day's theme and the provided Bible verse, taking a moment to meditate on its meaning and relevance to your life. Then, read the written prayer aloud or silently, making it your own. Feel free to pause, add your own words, or adapt the prayer to your specific circumstances.

After the prayer, take time to ponder the reflection question. This question is designed to deepen your understanding of the day's theme and help you apply it to your life. Consider journaling your thoughts or discussing them with a prayer partner. Use the written prayer and reflection question as a springboard for your own conversation with God, sharing your personal concerns, gratitude, and desires with Him. Try to keep the day's theme and verse in mind as you go about your daily activities, looking for ways to apply what you've learned and prayed about.

The reflection questions at the end of each day's entry are a crucial component of this devotional. They serve to encourage personal application, bridging the gap between biblical truth and everyday life.

These questions prompt you to examine your heart, attitudes, and behaviors in light of God's Word, which is vital for spiritual growth. Some questions may inspire you to take concrete actions or make changes in your life based on what you've prayed about. By pondering these questions, you'll gain a deeper understanding of God's Word and His will for your life. Additionally, these questions can serve as excellent conversation starters for Bible study groups or prayer partnerships, allowing you to share your spiritual journey with others.

Remember, this book is a tool to enhance your relationship with God, not a rigid formula. Feel free to adapt its use to best suit your spiritual needs and lifestyle. Some days, you may spend more time in reflection, while others might call for extended periods of prayer. The goal is to cultivate a consistent, meaningful prayer life that draws you closer to God and strengthens you for your daily walk.

As you journey through this year of prayer, may you experience God's presence in new and profound ways, finding the daily strength and guidance you need in Him. This devotional is designed to be a faithful companion in your spiritual growth, helping you navigate the joys and challenges of life with a prayerful heart and a deepening faith.

Week 1: Trusting God for the New Year

Day 1: SURRENDER TO GOD'S PLAN

"Trust in the Lord with all your heart and lean not on your own understanding"
(Proverbs 3:5, NIV)

Heavenly Father, I come before You with an open heart. Today, I choose to surrender my plans, my hopes, and my fears to You. Help me to release control and truly trust in Your perfect plan for my life. When I'm tempted to rely on my own wisdom, remind me of Your infinite knowledge and love.

Guide my steps, Lord, and help me to walk in faith, even when I can't see the path ahead. May this year be one of deep trust and surrender to Your will. Teach me to find peace in knowing that Your plans for me are far greater than anything I could imagine for myself. In Jesus' name, Amen.

What area of your life do you find most difficult to surrender to God's plan?

Day 2: FIND PEACE IN GOD'S SOVEREIGNTY

"And we know that in all things God works for the good of those who love him"
(Romans 8:28, NIV)

Lord God, help me to find peace in Your sovereignty, knowing that You are in control of every situation. When circumstances seem chaotic or overwhelming, remind me of Your overarching plan. Grant me the serenity to accept the things I cannot change, knowing that You are working all things for my good and Your glory.

Teach me to rest in the knowledge of Your sovereign control, even when life doesn't make sense to me. Help me to trust that Your ways are higher than my ways, and Your thoughts, higher than my thoughts. Let this trust be the foundation of an unshakeable peace in my life. In Your mighty name, I pray. Amen.

In what situation do you need to trust God's sovereignty more fully today?

"Now faith is confidence in what we hope for and assurance about what we do not see"
(Hebrews 11:1, NIV)

Faithful God, I ask You to increase my faith. Help me to trust in Your promises, even when I can't see their fulfillment. Strengthen my confidence in Your goodness and Your plan for my life. When doubts creep in, remind me of Your faithfulness in the past.

May my faith grow deeper and stronger with each passing day. Let my life be a testimony to Your trustworthiness. Teach me to walk by faith and not by sight, trusting in Your unseen hand guiding my life. Help me to step out in faith when You call, knowing that You will provide everything I need. In the name of Jesus, who is the author and perfecter of my faith, I pray. Amen.

What step of faith is God calling you to take in this new year?

Day 4: EMBRACE GOD'S PROMISES

"For no matter how many promises God has made, they are 'Yes' in Christ"
(2 Corinthians 1:20, NIV)

Gracious Father, when I feel weak, remind me of Your promise to be my strength. When I feel alone, help me remember Your promise to never leave me. When I'm anxious, bring to mind Your promise of peace. May Your promises be the foundation of my hope and the source of my courage.

Help me to stand firm on Your word, trusting in Your unfailing love and faithfulness. Teach me to meditate on Your promises day and night, allowing them to shape my thoughts, attitudes, and actions. Let Your promises be a light to my path and a guide for my decisions. May I live in the fullness of all that You have promised, experiencing the abundant life You offer. In Jesus' name, Amen.

Which of God's promises do you need to cling to most in this season of your life?

"When I am afraid, I put my trust in you"
(Psalm 56:3, NIV)

Almighty God, I confess my fears to You. But Lord, I choose to trust You instead of giving in to these fears. You are greater than any challenge I may face. Fill me with Your perfect love that casts out all fear. Help me to remember Your past faithfulness and to trust in Your future provision.

May my faith in You be stronger than any fear that tries to overtake me. Teach me to see my fears as opportunities to trust You more deeply. When anxiety threatens to overwhelm me, help me to turn to You in prayer, casting all my cares upon You. Let Your peace guard my heart and mind, replacing fear with confidence in Your unfailing love and care. In the powerful name of Jesus, I pray. Amen.

What fear do you need to surrender to God and replace with trust?

Day 6: SEEK GOD'S GUIDANCE

"In all your ways submit to him, and he will make your paths straight"
(Proverbs 3:6, NIV)

Wise and loving Father, thank you for the promise that You will make my paths straight. I humbly seek Your guidance for the year ahead. Direct my steps, Lord. Help me to discern Your will in every decision I face. When I'm unsure which way to turn, illuminate the path You want me to take. Give me the courage to follow Your leading, even when it doesn't make sense to my human understanding.

Teach me to listen for Your voice in prayer, in Your Word, and in the counsel of godly friends. Help me to be patient when Your direction isn't immediately clear, trusting that You will reveal the next step in Your perfect timing. Let every choice I make be an opportunity to honor You and further Your kingdom. In Jesus' name, I pray. Amen.

In what area of your life do you most need God's guidance right now?

"Jesus Christ is the same yesterday and today and forever"
(Hebrews 13:8, NIV)

Eternal God, how wonderful it is to think that Jesus Christ is the same yesterday, today, and forever! As I begin this new year, help me to anchor my hope in Your immutable nature. When everything around me seems unstable, remind me of Your constant love and faithfulness. May I find rest in knowing that Your character never changes, Your promises never fail, and Your love never diminishes.

Help me to build my life on the solid rock of Your unchanging truth. Teach me to rely on Your unchanging character rather than on my fluctuating emotions or circumstances. May my trust in Your unchanging nature lead me to a place of deep peace and unshakeable faith. In the name of Jesus, my unchanging Savior, I pray. Amen.

**How can remembering God's unchanging nature bring
you comfort in a particular situation you're facing?**

Week 2. Setting Godly Goals and Aspirations

Day 8: ALIGN DESIRES WITH GOD'S WILL

"Delight yourself in the Lord, and he will give you the desires of your heart"
(Psalm 37:4, ESV)

Loving Father, I come to You today with a heart full of desires and dreams. Your Word tells me to delight in You, and You will give me the desires of my heart. Help me to find my greatest joy in You, Lord. Let my desires align with Your will, knowing that You know what is best for me. Teach me to put my trust in Your plans, finding joy in the journey You have set before me.

May my ambitions be rooted in a desire to serve You and others rather than just seeking personal gain. Let my heart be content in the knowledge that You provide all I need when I delight in You, shaping my goals to reflect Your purpose and glory.

How can you align your desires with God's will today?

Day 9: PRIORITIZE SPIRITUAL GROWTH

"But grow in the grace and knowledge of our Lord and Savior Jesus Christ"
(2 Peter 3:18, NIV)

Heavenly Father, as I focus on setting goals for this year, I seek to prioritize my spiritual growth above all. Help me to grow in grace and deepen my understanding of Your Word, drawing closer to You each day. Let my heart be open to Your teachings, eager to learn and apply Your truths in my life. May my relationship with You be the foundation of all my aspirations.

Lord, guide me in creating a routine that nourishes my spirit and keeps me rooted in Your love. Encourage me to spend time in prayer and study, allowing Your wisdom to shape my thoughts and actions. Also, help me to encourage others on their journeys, sharing the grace and knowledge of our Lord and Savior, Jesus Christ.

How can you prioritize your spiritual growth today?

Day 10: SET MEANINGFUL GOALS

"May he give you the desire of your heart and make all your plans succeed"
(Psalm 20:4, NIV)

God of purpose, I thank You for the plans You have for my life. As I set goals for this season, I ask for Your guidance. May the desires of my heart align with Your will. Give me wisdom to discern which goals are truly meaningful in light of eternity.

Lord, I lay my plans before You. Bless the work of my hands and make my efforts fruitful. When obstacles arise, grant me perseverance. Help me to remember that my ultimate goal is to glorify You in all I do. Let my ambitions be guided by Your spirit, trusting that You will provide the resources and opportunities I need to succeed. May the goals I pursue draw me closer to You and make me more effective in serving others. In Jesus' name, Amen.

What God-honoring goal do you feel led to pursue?

"If any of you lacks wisdom, you should ask God, who gives generously to all"
(James 1:5, NIV)

All-wise God, I stand in awe of Your perfect wisdom. As I face decisions, both big and small, I recognize my need for Your guidance. Your Word promises that if I lack wisdom, I can ask You, and You will give generously. Today, I humbly seek Your wisdom.

Illuminate my mind, Lord. Help me to see situations from Your perspective. Guard me against hasty judgments or selfish motivations. When I'm unsure, teach me to wait patiently for Your leading. May every choice I make be an opportunity to honor You and to walk in Your ways. Thank You for Your willingness to guide me. In Jesus' name, Amen.

What decision are you currently facing that you need to bring before God?

Day 12: BALANCE AMBITION AND CONTENTMENT

"I know what it is to be in need, and I know what it is to have plenty"
(Philippians 4:12, NIV)

Dear Lord, as I pursue my goals and dreams, help me to find the balance between ambition and contentment. I confess that I often struggle with this balance. Sometimes, I'm overly ambitious, always wanting more. Other times, I lack the drive to use my gifts fully. Help me find the right balance. Teach me to strive for excellence while being grateful for what I have.

May my heart be open to Your leading, trusting that You will provide for my needs at the right time and in the right way. Let my desire for more never overshadow my gratitude for Your blessings. May I work diligently as unto You, while trusting You with the results. Grant me the wisdom to know when to strive and when to rest in Your sufficiency. In Jesus' name, Amen.

In what area of your life do you need to find a better
balance between ambition and contentment?

"There is a time for everything, and a season for every activity under the heavens"
(Ecclesiastes 3:1, NIV)

Eternal God, Your Word reminds me that there is a time for everything under heaven. Yet, I often grow impatient, wanting things to happen on my schedule. Forgive my impatience, Lord, and help me trust Your perfect timing. When doors seem closed, give me the faith to wait on Your opening. When opportunities arise unexpectedly, grant me the courage to step out in faith. '

Help me to remember that Your timing is always perfect, even when I don't understand it. May I inspire others to find peace in waiting on You. Teach me to cherish each season, knowing that Your timing always brings about what is best for me. In Jesus' name, Amen.

What situation in your life requires you to trust God's timing?

Day 14: CULTIVATE PERSEVERANCE

"Let us not become weary in doing good, for at the proper
time we will reap a harvest if we do not give up"
(Galatians 6:9, NIV)

Dear Lord, I ask for the strength to persevere in doing good. Help me to stay committed to the tasks You have set before me, even when the journey becomes challenging. Remind me that every effort made in Your name is not in vain, and that You see and honor the work of my hands. Guide me to find encouragement in Your promises when I feel weary.

Let the hope of reaping a future harvest motivate me to press on. Fill my heart with patience and endurance, trusting that You are working behind the scenes to bring about a fruitful season in Your perfect timing. May my actions reflect a steadfast faith in Your promises. Help me to uplift those around me, sharing the assurance that perseverance in goodness leads to a rich reward.

What area of your life requires perseverance so
that you may see the harvest God promises?

Day 15: RECOGNIZE GOD'S LOVE IN CREATION

"For since the creation of the world God's invisible qualities—
his eternal power and divine nature—have been clearly seen"
(Romans 1:20, NIV)

Gracious Creator, as I look around at the beauty of the world, I am reminded of Your immense love and power. The mountains, oceans, and skies all speak of Your divine nature and creativity. Help me to see Your hand at work in every part of creation.

Teach me to pause and appreciate the intricate details of the world You have made. In the gentle rustle of leaves and the vibrant colors of a sunset, let me see the evidence of Your care and attention. Open my eyes to the countless ways You reveal Yourself through nature, and let these reflections deepen my love for You and the world around me.

What aspect of God's creation particularly speaks to you about His love?

Day 16: EXPERIENCE GOD'S LOVE THROUGH SCRIPTURE

"Your word is a lamp for my feet, a light on my path"
(Psalm 119:105, NIV)

Loving Father, as I open Your Word, I am reminded of the profound love You have for me. Teach me to seek Your guidance through the pages of the Bible, finding comfort and direction in its truths. When I am faced with uncertainty, may I turn to Your Word and find peace in its promises. Let the stories and teachings within inspire me to live a life that honors You and reflects Your love to those around me.

Let me carry Your light into the world, sharing the hope and love your word provides with others. Inspire me to encourage those around me to discover the treasure of Your Word, helping them to experience the depth of Your love through its teachings.

Which passage of Scripture has recently helped
you experience God's love more deeply?

"Dear friends, let us love one another, for love comes from God"
(1 John 4:7, NIV)

Heavenly Father, today, I am reminded of the call to share your love with those around me. Help me to reflect Your love in my interactions, showing kindness and compassion to everyone I meet. May my actions and words be a testament to the love that You have so freely given, inspiring others to seek You through the love they experience in their own lives.

Teach me to love without conditions, just as You have loved me. When faced with difficult situations or challenging people, remind me of the grace and patience You have shown. Let Your love guide my responses, transforming my heart to be more like Yours each day. May I be a vessel of Your love, bringing light to the lives of those I encounter.

How can you show God's love to someone in your life today?

Day 18: GOD'S UNCONDITIONAL LOVE

"Neither height nor depth, nor anything else in all creation,
will be able to separate us from the love of God"
(Romans 8:39, NIV)

Eternal God, in moments of doubt or insecurity, help me to find deep comfort in this truth. Your love for me is not based on my performance or worthiness, but on Your unchanging character. When I feel unlovable, remind me that You love me unconditionally.

When I stumble, assure me that Your love remains steadfast. Guide me to embrace the depth of Your love in every aspect of my life. When I feel unworthy or distant, draw me back with gentle reminders of Your grace. Help me to rest in the assurance that Your love is not based on my actions, but on who You are—a loving and faithful God.

How can you remind yourself of God's unconditional
love when you're feeling insecure?

*"See what great love the Father has lavished on us,
that we should be called children of God!"*
(1 John 3:1, NIV)

Heavenly Father, as I struggle with self-doubt, remind me of the incredible love You have poured out on me. Your love is unchanging and calls me Your child, giving me a new identity rooted in Your grace. Help me to see myself through Your eyes, embracing the truth of who I am in You, rather than the lies of insecurity.

Guide me to stand firm in the knowledge of Your love, especially when doubts and fears try to overshadow my worth. Teach me to let go of negative thoughts and replace them with the assurance of being loved unconditionally by You. May Your love be the foundation that strengthens my confidence and renews my spirit each day. Amen.

**How can you overcome self-doubt today by embracing y
our identity as a beloved child of God?**

Day 20: EMBRACE GOD'S LOVE IN TRIALS

"And so we know and rely on the love God has for us"
(1 John 4:16, NIV)

Faithful God, Your Word assures me that I can know and rely on the love You have for me. As I face trials and challenges, help me to embrace Your love as my anchor. When circumstances are difficult, remind me that Your love for me remains constant.

Give me the faith to trust that You are working all things for my good, even when I can't see it. Help me to feel Your loving presence in the midst of my struggles. May the assurance of Your unfailing love give me strength to endure and hope to persevere. Let these trials deepen my understanding and appreciation of Your great love for me. In Jesus' name, Amen.

How has God's love sustained you in a recent trial?

"Draw near to God, and he will draw near to you."
(James 4:8, ESV)

Heavenly Father, help me to prioritize time in Your presence, setting aside distractions to focus on the beauty of being with You. Let my heart long for the closeness that comes from a relationship built on faith and love. May my soul find rest and joy in the assurance that You are near.

Guide me to create habits that draw me closer to You each day. Whether through prayer, meditation, or reading Your Word, let these moments become the foundation of my relationship with You. Teach me to listen for Your voice and recognize Your guidance in my life. May I be open to Your leading, allowing Your love to transform my heart and mind.

**How can you draw nearer to God today and cultivate
a more loving relationship with Him?**

Week 4. Cultivating Inner Strength and Resilience

Day 22: DRAW STRENGTH FROM GOD'S WORD

"I can do all this through him who gives me strength."
(Philippians 4:13, NIV)

Heavenly Father, I come before You today, seeking the strength that only You can provide. Your Word assures me that I can do all things through Christ who strengthens me. As I face the challenges of this day, help me to draw upon this promise, finding courage and resilience in Your unfailing power.

Lord, there are times when I feel overwhelmed by the tasks before me, doubting my abilities and questioning my purpose. In these moments of weakness, remind me that Your strength is made perfect in my inadequacies. Help me to lean not on my own understanding but to trust fully in Your wisdom and guidance.

How can you rely on God's strength rather than your own today?

"The Lord is close to the brokenhearted and saves those who are crushed in spirit"
(Psalm 34:18, NIV)

Father, life's hardships often leave me feeling fragile. I'm grateful that You're always near, especially when my heart aches. Help me find stability in Your unchanging love, even when everything else seems uncertain. Let Your presence be my anchor in the storms of life, keeping me steady when emotions threaten to overwhelm me.

There are days when my feelings seem too intense to bear – fear, anger, or sadness threaten to take over. During these times, draw me close to You. Shape me into a person of strength, able to handle emotional challenges with grace and hope.

How can you create a safe space to express your emotions to God today?

Day 24: OVERCOME OBSTACLES WITH FAITH

"I have told you these things, so that in me you may have peace. In this world you will have trouble. But take heart! I have overcome the world"
(John 16:33, NIV)

Jesus, You've warned us that life won't always be easy, but You've also promised us Your peace. When I face seemingly insurmountable obstacles, help me remember that You've already conquered them all. Let Your victory be the source of my courage, empowering me to face each challenge with confidence in Your overcoming power.

When I'm discouraged, remind me how You've guided me through difficult situations before. Let my faith in You grow stronger with each hurdle I overcome. Lord, I ask for the faith to trust You even when I can't see the way forward. Amen.

What obstacle in your life can you entrust to God's care today?

"But those who hope in the Lord will renew their strength."
(Isaiah 40:31, NIV)

Almighty God, just as athletes train their bodies, I want to build my spiritual endurance. Let my hope in You be the source of my strength. Help me to cultivate spiritual disciplines that will sustain me through both calm and stormy seasons.

Sometimes, my spiritual life feels stagnant, and my devotional practices become routine. Rekindle my passion for You, Lord. Help me approach each day with fresh expectancy, eager to see what new things You will do. May my spiritual stamina grow, enabling me to run this race of faith with perseverance. Amen.

What spiritual practice can you engage in today to build your spiritual stamina?

Day 26: FIND STRENGTH IN COMMUNITY

"Two are better than one, because they have a good return for their labor"
(Ecclesiastes 4:9, NIV)

Loving Father, thank You for the gift of community. Help me nurture meaningful relationships that support and encourage my faith journey. It's tempting to isolate myself, thinking I can handle everything on my own. Give me the humility to ask for help when I need it, and the compassion to support others in their struggles.

Teach me to be authentic in my relationships. Help me to see the value in diverse perspectives and experiences within my community. Show me how to be a good friend, a supportive family member, and a valuable part of my church. Help me to use my gifts to strengthen the body of Christ, and to receive with gratitude the gifts that others bring.

Who in your community can you reach out to today,
either for support or to offer encouragement?

"Finally, brothers and sisters, whatever is true, whatever is noble, whatever is right, whatever is pure, whatever is lovely, whatever is admirable— if anything is excellent or praiseworthy—think about such things"
(Philippians 4:8, NIV)

Heavenly Father, shape my thoughts to reflect Your goodness. Help me see the world through Your eyes of love and hope. Transform my mind so that positivity becomes my default perspective. Help me notice the beauty and goodness that surrounds me each day.

Forgive me for allowing pessimism to cloud my view. Teach me to practice gratitude, acknowledging Your blessings and the kindness of others. Let my positive outlook be a light in dark places, drawing others to the hope found in You. Transform my thought patterns, Lord, that I might be renewed day by day, growing in the likeness of Christ.

What is one positive thought you can focus on throughout your day?

Day 28: TRUST GOD'S STRENGTH IN WEAKNESS

"But he said to me, 'My grace is sufficient for you, for my power is made perfect in weakness'"
(2 Corinthians 12:9, NIV)

Gracious God, I often try to hide my weaknesses, but You see them as opportunities. Help me embrace my limitations, knowing that they allow Your strength to shine through me more clearly. Give me the courage to be honest about my struggles, both with You and with others.

When I feel inadequate or overwhelmed, remind me that Your power isn't diminished by my shortcomings. Instead, teach me to find freedom in depending on Your grace. May my vulnerabilities become channels for Your strength to flow, showing others the sufficiency of Your love. Amen.

In what area of weakness can you invite God's strength today?

Day 29: FOSTER OPEN COMMUNICATION

"Let your conversation be always full of grace, seasoned with salt"
(Colossians 4:6, NIV)

Heavenly Father, Your Word teaches us to let our conversation be full of grace. Help me to communicate openly and honestly with my family and friends. Give me the wisdom to choose words that build up rather than tear down and the courage to speak truth in love.

Lord, there are times when I struggle to express myself clearly or to listen attentively to others. Teach me to be a better communicator and a more patient listener. Help me to create an environment where others feel safe to share their thoughts and feelings openly. Amen.

**How can you improve your communication
with a family member or friend today?**

Day 30: PRACTICE FORGIVENESS AND GRACE

*"Bear with each other and forgive one another if any of you has
a grievance against someone. Forgive as the Lord forgave you"*
(Colossians 3:13, NIV)

Merciful God, You have shown me immeasurable grace and forgiveness through Christ. Help me to extend that same forgiveness and grace to my family and friends. When I'm hurt or offended, remind me of the forgiveness You've granted me. Help me to release bitterness and embrace the freedom that comes with forgiveness.

Teach me to be quick to forgive and slow to take offense. May Your grace flow through me, bringing healing to strained relationships and reflecting Your love to those around me. Help me to be an agent of reconciliation in my family and among my friends. In Jesus' name, I pray. Amen.

**Is there someone you need to forgive or from
whom you need to seek forgiveness?**

"How good and pleasant it is when God's people live together in unity!"
(Psalm 133:1, NIV)

Loving Father, Your Word reminds us how good and pleasant it is when Your people dwell together in unity. Help me to prioritize quality time with my family and friends. In our busy world, remind me of the importance of nurturing these relationships.

Lord, show me creative ways to spend meaningful time with my loved ones. Whether it's sharing a meal, engaging in conversation, or enjoying activities together, help me to be fully present in these moments. Teach me to put aside distractions and truly connect with those You've placed in my life. Help us to create lasting memories and deepen our relationships. In Jesus' name, I pray. Amen.

**What intentional step can you take to spend quality t
ime with a family member or friend this week?**

Day 32: SHOW LOVE THROUGH ACTIONS

"Dear children, let us not love with words or speech but with actions and in truth"
(1 John 3:18, NIV)

Gracious God, Your Word instructs us to love not just with words, but with actions and in truth. Help me to demonstrate my love for family and friends through tangible acts of kindness and service. Open my eyes to see the needs of those around me and give me a willing heart to meet those needs.

Lord, sometimes I get caught up in my own concerns and forget to show love to others. Forgive me for those times when I've been selfish or negligent. Teach me to be more observant and proactive in expressing love through my actions. In Jesus' name, I pray. Amen.

What specific act of love can you perform for a family member or friend today?

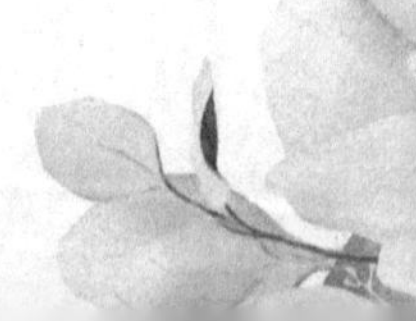

"Therefore encourage one another and build each other up, just as in fact you are doing"
(1 Thessalonians 5:11, NIV)

Heavenly Father, You call us to encourage one another and build each other up. Help me to be a source of encouragement to my family and friends. Give me eyes to see the best in others and the words to affirm their worth and potential. Teach me to speak words that inspire confidence and motivate growth in others.

May my presence in the lives of my loved ones be uplifting and edifying. Help me to celebrate their successes, comfort them in their struggles, and consistently point them towards You. Let my words and actions contribute to building a strong, supportive community among my family and friends. In Jesus' name, I pray. Amen.

Who in your life needs encouragement today, and how can you provide it?

Day 34: PRACTICE PATIENCE AND KINDNESS

"Love is patient, love is kind. It does not envy, it does not boast, it is not proud"
(1 Corinthians 13:4, NIV)

Loving God, Your Word teaches us that love is patient and kind. Help me to embody these qualities in my relationships with family and friends. When I'm tempted to be short-tempered or unkind, remind me of Your endless patience and kindness towards me. Give me the strength to respond with gentleness, even in frustrating situations.

May Your patience and kindness flow through me, Father. Let these qualities be evident in my words, actions, and even my thoughts towards others. Use me to create an atmosphere of love and acceptance in my home and among my friends. In Jesus' name, I pray. Amen.

In what situation do you need to practice more patience or kindness today?

*"And pray in the Spirit on all occasions with all kinds of prayers and requests.
With this in mind, be alert and always keep on praying for all the Lord's people"
(Ephesians 6:18, NIV)*

Gracious Father, Your Word encourages us to pray continually for all the Lord's people. Today, I lift up my family and friends to You. You know the needs, struggles, and desires of my loved ones better than I do. I ask for Your blessing and guidance in their lives. Protect them from harm, lead them in Your ways, and draw them closer to You. For those who don't know You, I pray that You would reveal Yourself to them.

Help me to be faithful in praying for my family and friends, Lord. Remind me to bring their concerns before You regularly. May my prayers be a source of spiritual support and a demonstration of my love for them. In Jesus' name, I pray. Amen.

Who among your family and friends can you commit to praying for regularly?

February

Week 6. Finding Purpose in God's Plan

Day 36: DISCOVER YOUR DIVINE CALLING

*"For we are God's handiwork, created in Christ Jesus to do good works, which God
prepared in advance for us to do" (Ephesians 2:10, NIV)*

Heavenly Father, I am in awe that You have created me with a purpose. Help me to discover the divine calling You have prepared for me. Open my eyes to see the good works You have destined me to accomplish. Give me the courage to step into the plans You have for my life.

Lord, guide me in understanding my unique gifts and talents. Show me how to use them for Your glory and the benefit of others. May I always remember that I am Your handiwork, carefully crafted for a specific purpose. In Jesus' name, I pray. Amen.

How can you start exploring God's purpose for your life today?

"Many are the plans in a person's heart, but it is the Lord's purpose that prevails"
(Proverbs 19:21, NIV)

Sovereign God, I acknowledge that Your purpose for my life is far greater than any plans I can make for myself. Help me to align my heart and my actions with Your divine will. When my desires conflict with Your plans, give me the wisdom and strength to surrender to Your purpose.

Father, teach me to seek Your guidance in all areas of my life. May I learn to discern Your voice and follow Your leading. Help me to trust in Your perfect plan, even when I don't understand it. Let Your purpose prevail in my life, and use me as an instrument of Your will. In Jesus' name, I pray. Amen.

In what area of your life do you need to surrender your plans to God's purpose?

Day 38: EMBRACE YOUR UNIQUE GIFTS

"We have different gifts, according to the grace given to each of us"
(Romans 12:6, NIV)

Gracious Father, thank You for blessing me with unique gifts. Help me to recognize and appreciate the special abilities You have given me. Remove any doubts or insecurities that prevent me from fully embracing these gifts. Give me the confidence to use them for Your glory.

Lord, show me how to develop and refine the talents You've entrusted to me. Guide me in using these gifts to serve others and further Your kingdom. May I always remember that my abilities are a reflection of Your grace in my life. Help me to steward them well and use them to honor You. In Jesus' name, I pray. Amen.

What unique gift has God given you, and how can you use it to serve others?

*"Trust in the Lord with all your heart and lean not on your own understanding;
in all your ways submit to him, and he will make your paths straight"*
(Proverbs 3:5–6, NIV)

Wise and loving God, I come to You seeking guidance in my decisions. Help me to trust in You completely, rather than relying on my own limited understanding. Give me the humility to submit all my ways to You, knowing that Your wisdom far surpasses my own.

Father, when I face crossroads in life, big or small, remind me to turn to You first. Open my heart to hear Your voice, and grant me discernment to recognize Your leading. As I follow Your guidance, I trust that You will make my paths straight. May all my decisions align with Your perfect will for my life. In Jesus' name, I pray. Amen.

What decision are you facing that you need to bring before God?

Day 40: FIND JOY IN SERVING OTHERS

*"Each of you should use whatever gift you have received to serve others,
as faithful stewards of God's grace in its various forms."*
(1 Peter 4:10, NIV)

Loving Father, thank You for the gifts You have given me and the opportunity to serve others. Help me to be a faithful steward of Your grace, using my abilities to bless those around me. Fill my heart with joy as I serve, reminding me that in serving others, I am serving You.

Lord, open my eyes to see the needs of those around me. Give me creativity and wisdom in using my gifts to meet those needs. May I serve with humility and love, reflecting Your character in all I do. Let my service be a testament to Your grace and a source of encouragement to others. In Jesus' name, I pray. Amen.

How can you use your gifts to serve someone in need today?

"I press on toward the goal to win the prize for which
God has called me heavenward in Christ Jesus"
(Philippians 3:14, NIV)

Mighty God, I thank You for the purpose You have given me in Christ Jesus. When I face obstacles that hinder me from fulfilling this purpose, grant me the strength and determination to press on. Help me to keep my eyes fixed on the prize of Your heavenly calling.

Father, when discouragement or doubt creeps in, remind me of Your faithfulness. Give me perseverance to push through challenges and wisdom to navigate difficulties. May I always remember that with You, all things are possible. Empower me to overcome every obstacle that stands in the way of Your purpose for my life. In Jesus' name, I pray. Amen.

What obstacle to your purpose do you need God's help to overcome?

Day 42: LIVE WITH ETERNAL PERSPECTIVE

"Set your minds on things above, not on earthly things."
(Colossians 3:2, NIV)

Eternal Father, help me to set my mind on heavenly things and live with an eternal perspective. In a world that constantly draws my attention to temporary concerns, remind me of what truly matters in light of eternity. Guide my thoughts, decisions, and actions to align with Your eternal purposes.

Lord, when I'm tempted to become overly focused on earthly matters, redirect my gaze to You. Help me to prioritize what has eternal significance in my life. May I invest my time, resources, and energy in ways that have lasting impact for Your kingdom. In Jesus' name, Amen.

How can you shift your focus from temporary concerns to eternal matters today?

Day 43: GOD'S UNCONDITIONAL LOVE

*"This is love: not that we loved God, but that he loved us
and sent his Son as an atoning sacrifice for our sins"*
(1 John 4:10, NIV)

Heavenly Father, I am overwhelmed by the depth of Your unconditional love. Thank You for loving me first, even when I was undeserving. Help me to truly grasp the magnitude of Your love demonstrated through Christ's sacrifice for my sins.

Lord, let the reality of Your unconditional love transform my heart and mind. May it shape how I view myself and others. Teach me to receive Your love fully and to extend it to those around me. Let Your love be the foundation of my faith and the driving force in my life. In Jesus' name, I pray. Amen.

How can you reflect God's unconditional love to someone today?

Day 44: SELF-LOVE THROUGH GOD'S EYES

"I praise you because I am fearfully and wonderfully made."
(Psalm 139:14, NIV)

Loving Creator, I thank You for making me fearfully and wonderfully. Help me to see myself through Your eyes, appreciating the unique way You've crafted me. When I struggle with self-doubt or criticism, remind me of Your perfect design in creating me.

Father, guide me in cultivating a healthy self-love that's rooted in Your love for me. Help me to embrace my strengths and weaknesses, knowing that You use all aspects of who I am for Your purpose. May I treat myself with the same kindness and respect that You show me. In Jesus' name, I pray. Amen.

**What aspect of yourself do you need to start
appreciating as God's wonderful creation?**

"Love your neighbor as yourself."
(Mark 12:31, NIV)

Compassionate God, You call me to love my neighbor as myself. Give me a heart that truly cares for others, seeing them as You see them. Help me to extend the same grace, kindness, and understanding to others that I desire for myself. Remind me of your great love for me so that I can truly love others as well, even when they seem unlovable in my own eyes.

Lord, open my eyes to the needs of those around me. Give me wisdom to know how to love them practically and meaningfully. When it's challenging to love certain individuals, remind me of Your unconditional love for all. May my love for others be a testament to Your love working through me. In Jesus' name, I pray. Amen.

Who is a "neighbor" in your life that you can show love to today?

Day 46: PRACTICE SACRIFICIAL LOVE

"Greater love has no one than this: to lay down one's life for one's friends"
(John 15:13, NIV)

Selfless Savior, You demonstrated the ultimate sacrificial love by laying down Your life for us. Teach me to love others with that same selfless attitude. Give me the courage to put others' needs before my own, even when it's costly or uncomfortable.

Father, show me practical ways to practice sacrificial love in my daily life. Help me to give my time, resources, and energy for the benefit of others. When I'm tempted to hold back, remind me of Christ's sacrifice for me. May my sacrificial love be a powerful witness of Your love to those around me. In Jesus' name, I pray. Amen.

In what area of your life is God calling you to practice more sacrificial love?

"And so we know and rely on the love God has for us. God is love."
(1 John 4:16, NIV)

Eternal God, You are love itself. Help me wrap my head around that reality: You are Love. You are overflowing with love, and You delight in pouring that wonderful, immeasurable love into my heart. When I face difficult times, help me to know and rely on Your unfailing love. Let Your love be my anchor in the storms of life, my comfort in sorrow, and my hope in despair.

Father, in moments when I struggle to feel Your love, remind me of its constancy. Help me to trust in Your love even when circumstances are challenging. May Your love sustain me, strengthen me, and guide me through every trial. Let my confidence in Your love grow deeper with each passing day. In Jesus' name, I pray. Amen.

How can you remind yourself of God's love during challenging times?

Day 48: EXTEND LOVE TO ENEMIES

"But I tell you, love your enemies and pray for those who persecute you"
(Matthew 5:44, NIV)

Merciful Father, You call me to the challenging task of loving my enemies. Give me the strength and grace to love those who have hurt me or oppose me. Help me to see them through Your eyes of compassion and to respond to them with Your love.

Lord, when I struggle with feelings of anger or resentment, soften my heart. Teach me to pray sincerely for those who have wronged me. Let Your love flow through me, breaking down barriers and healing relationships. May my love for my enemies be a powerful testimony of Your transforming love. In Jesus' name, I pray. Amen.

**Who is someone you find difficult to love, a
nd how can you start praying for them?**

"Above all, love each other deeply, because love covers over a multitude of sins"
(1 Peter 4:8, NIV)

Gracious God, thank You for the relationships You've blessed me with. Help me to nurture deep, genuine love in these relationships. Teach me to love others not just in word, but in action and in truth.

Father, give me patience and understanding in my relationships. When conflicts arise, remind me that love covers a multitude of sins. Help me to forgive readily, extend grace generously, and always seek the good of others. May the love in my relationships reflect Your enduring love for us. Let my relationships be a source of joy, growth, and mutual encouragement. In Jesus' name, I pray. Amen.

How can you demonstrate deep love in one of your key relationships today?

Week 8. Praying for Leaders and Authorities

Day 50: INTERCEDE FOR NATIONAL LEADERS

"I urge, then, first of all, that petitions, prayers, intercession and thanksgiving
be made for all people—for kings and all those in authority"
(1 Timothy 2:1-2, NIV)

Sovereign Lord, You call us to pray for all people, especially those in positions of authority. Today, I lift up our national leaders to You. Grant them wisdom, integrity, and compassion as they govern our nation. Guide their decisions and actions to align with Your will.

Father, help me to faithfully intercede for our leaders, regardless of my personal opinions or political leanings. Give me a heart of thanksgiving for the responsibility they bear. May my prayers contribute to creating an environment where peace and godliness can flourish in our nation. In Jesus' name, I pray. Amen.

How can you make praying for national leaders a regular part of your prayer life?

"Give the king your justice, O God, and your righteousness to the royal son!"
(Psalm 72:1, ESV)

Wise and Just God, I pray for those who govern our land. Pour out Your wisdom upon them, that they may lead with justice and righteousness. Grant them discernment to make decisions that honor You and benefit all people.

Lord, when our leaders face complex challenges, be their guiding light. Help them to seek Your counsel and to govern with fairness and compassion. May Your justice and righteousness be evident in the laws and policies of our land. Let our leaders be known for their wisdom and integrity. In Jesus' name, I pray. Amen.

In what specific area do our leaders need God's wisdom today?

Day 52: SUPPORT LEADERS WITH PRAYER

"Also, seek the peace and prosperity of the city to which I have carried you into exile.
Pray to the Lord for it, because if it prospers, you too will prosper"
(Jeremiah 29:7, NIV)

Heavenly Father, You instruct us to pray for the peace and prosperity of our communities and nations. Today, I lift up our local and national leaders, asking that You would guide them in fostering peace and promoting prosperity for all.

Lord, help me to be faithful in supporting our leaders through prayer, even when I disagree with their decisions. Give our leaders vision and strategies that will lead to the flourishing of our society. May their efforts result in justice, equality, and opportunity for all citizens. Let my prayers contribute to the well-being of our nation. In Jesus' name, I pray. Amen.

How can you actively support your community
leaders through prayer this week?

*"When the righteous increase, the people rejoice,
but when the wicked rule, the people groan"
(Proverbs 29:2, ESV)*

Righteous God, Your Word teaches us the impact of righteous leadership. I pray for an increase of righteousness among our leaders at all levels of government. Raise up men and women of integrity who will lead with justice, compassion, and fear of You. Please touch the hearts of our leaders today. Give them strength and wisdom to lead our country and our community.

Father, where there is corruption or wickedness in leadership, I pray for transformation. Touch the hearts of our leaders, drawing them to Your truth and righteousness. Give our citizens wisdom in choosing leaders of good character. May our nation rejoice because of righteous leadership that reflects Your values. In Jesus' name, I pray. Amen.

How can you promote and support righteous leadership in your community?

Day 54: INTERCEDE FOR PEACE AND JUSTICE

*"Righteousness and justice are the foundation of your throne;
love and faithfulness go before you"
(Psalm 89:14, NIV)*

Just and Loving God, Your throne is established on righteousness and justice. I pray for these qualities to be manifest in the leadership and governance of our nation. Guide our leaders in establishing and upholding laws that promote peace and ensure justice for all.

Lord, where there is injustice or conflict in our society, I ask for Your intervention. Give our leaders the wisdom to address root causes and the courage to stand for what is right. May love and faithfulness characterize their actions and decisions. Please clear up their visions, allowing them to understand other people's perspectives. Amen.

What specific issue of peace or justice can you intercede for today?

"How good and pleasant it is when God's people live together in unity!"
(Psalm 133:1, NIV)

God of Unity, You delight when Your people dwell in harmony. I pray for unity among our leaders across political, ideological, and cultural divides. Help them to find common ground and work together for the good of all. Help them to remember that our community had elected them to do the right thing.

Father, where there is division or partisan conflict, I ask for Your peace to prevail. Give our leaders hearts of humility and mutual respect. Help them to listen to one another and to seek collaborative solutions. May their unity be a powerful testimony to our nation and the world. Let their shared purpose in serving the people overcome their differences. In Jesus' name, I pray. Amen.

How can you promote unity and overcome division
in your own sphere of influence?

Day 56: SEEK GOD'S GUIDANCE FOR LEADERS

"For lack of guidance a nation falls, but victory is won through many advisers"
(Proverbs 11:14, NIV)

All-knowing God, Your guidance is essential for the success of any nation. I pray that our leaders would seek Your wisdom and surround themselves with godly advisers. Grant them humility to acknowledge their need for divine guidance and wise counsel.

Lord, I ask that You would raise up advisers of integrity and wisdom to support our leaders. Give our leaders discernment to recognize and heed good advice. May they always turn to You as their ultimate source of guidance. Let Your will be done through the decisions and policies they implement. Guide our nation on the path of righteousness and prosperity. In Jesus' name, I pray. Amen.

Which specific leader would you like to pray for today?

Day 57: RECOGNIZE YOUR WORTH IN GOD

"You are altogether beautiful, my darling; there is no flaw in you"
(Song of Songs 4:7, NIV)

Loving Father, I come before You today, seeking to truly understand and embrace my worth in Your eyes. Help me to see myself as You see me - altogether beautiful and without flaw. When I struggle with self-doubt or feelings of inadequacy, remind me of Your perfect love and acceptance.

Lord, I pray for the strength to reject the world's standards of worth and beauty. Instead, help me to find my value in being Your beloved daughter. May I walk in confidence, knowing that I am fearfully and wonderfully made by You. Amen.

How can you remind yourself of your worth in God's eyes today?

Day 58: EMBRACE YOUR UNIQUE CALLING

"Before I formed you in the womb I knew you, before you were born I set you apart"
(Jeremiah 1:5, NIV)

Sovereign God, I am in awe of Your intimate knowledge of me. You knew me before I was formed and set me apart for a unique purpose. Help me to embrace the calling You have placed on my life. Give me the courage to step into the plans You have prepared for me, even when they seem daunting or unclear.

Lord, I pray for discernment to recognize the gifts and talents You've given me. Show me how to use these abilities to fulfill my calling and glorify Your name. When I doubt my capabilities or question my path, remind me that You have equipped me for every good work You've prepared for me to do. In Jesus' name, I pray. Amen.

**What unique gifts has God given you, and how
can you use them to fulfill your calling?**

"Your beauty should not come from outward adornment...
Rather, it should be that of your inner self"
(1 Peter 3:3-4, NIV)

Gracious God, in a world that often prioritizes outward appearances, help me to focus on cultivating inner beauty. May my heart be adorned with the unfading beauty of a gentle and quiet spirit, which is of great worth in Your sight. Give me the wisdom to invest more in my character than in my outward appearance.

Lord, I pray for the fruit of Your Spirit to grow in my life - love, joy, peace, patience, kindness, goodness, faithfulness, gentleness, and self-control. Let these qualities shine through me, reflecting Your beauty to the world around me. When I'm tempted to find my worth in external things, redirect my focus to the development of my inner self. Amen.

What aspect of your inner beauty can you focus on developing today?

Day 60: STAND FIRM IN YOUR FAITH

"Be on your guard; stand firm in the faith; be courageous; be strong."
(1 Corinthians 16:13, NIV)

Almighty God, in a world that often challenges my beliefs, I pray for the strength to stand firm in my faith. Help me to be on guard against influences that would weaken my conviction or lead me astray. Grant me the courage to hold fast to Your truth, even when it's unpopular or difficult.

Lord, I ask for discernment to recognize spiritual attacks and the wisdom to combat them with Your Word. Strengthen my faith through regular study of Scripture, prayer, and fellowship with other believers. When doubts arise, or my faith is tested, remind me of Your faithfulness and the firm foundation I have in Christ. Amen.

In what area of your life do you need to stand firm in your faith today?

"She speaks with wisdom, and faithful instruction is on her tongue"
(Proverbs 31:26, NIV)

Wise and All-knowing God, I come before You seeking the wisdom that comes from above. Fill me with Your knowledge and understanding, that I may speak words of wisdom and offer faithful instruction to those around me. Help me to grow in godly wisdom each day, applying Your truth to every aspect of my life.

Lord, I pray for discernment to distinguish between worldly wisdom and Your divine wisdom. Guide my thoughts, words, and actions to align with Your will. When I face difficult decisions or challenging situations, remind me to seek Your wisdom first. May Your Word be a lamp to my feet and a light to my path. In Jesus' name, I pray. Amen.

How can you seek and apply God's wisdom in a specific situation you're facing?

Day 62: NURTURE A SERVANT'S HEART

"Whoever wants to become great among you must be your servant"
(Matthew 20:26, NIV)

Servant King, You have shown us the true meaning of greatness through Your life of service. I pray for a heart that reflects Your servant nature. Help me to see opportunities to serve others in my daily life, and give me the willingness to put others' needs before my own.

Lord, I ask for humility in my service. Guard me against serving for recognition or praise, but rather let me serve out of love for You and others. When serving becomes challenging or thankless, remind me of Your example and the eternal value of selfless love. May I find joy and fulfillment in following Your model of servanthood. Amen.

What is one way you can serve someone selflessly today?

Day 63: FIND STRENGTH IN SISTERHOOD

"Two are better than one, because they have a good return for their labor"
(Ecclesiastes 4:9, NIV)

Loving God, thank You for the gift of sisterhood and community. I pray for meaningful, supportive relationships with other women of faith. Help me to build and nurture friendships that encourage spiritual growth, offer mutual support, and glorify You.

Father, I pray that You would use the power of sisterhood to strengthen Your church and impact the world. Help me to be vulnerable and authentic in my relationships, creating space for others to do the same. May our collective strength as sisters in Christ be a testimony to Your love and a force for good in our communities. In Jesus' name, I pray. Amen.

**How can you strengthen your bonds of sisterhood
with other women of faith this week?**

March

Day 64: PRIORITIZE GOD FIRST

*"But seek first his kingdom and his righteousness,
and all these things will be given to you as well"*
(Matthew 6:33, NIV)

Heavenly Father, help me to prioritize You above all else. Guide me in seeking Your kingdom and righteousness first, trusting that You will provide for all my needs. When I'm tempted to put work, family, or other concerns before my relationship with You, remind me of the importance of keeping You at the center of my life.

Help me to align my goals and ambitions with Your will, finding fulfillment in pursuing Your purposes for my life. I pray that as I prioritize You, my family and work life will be blessed. Let my commitment to You inspire those around me to seek You as well. Amen.

How can you practically put God first in your daily routine?

"Teach us to number our days, that we may gain a heart of wisdom"
(Psalm 90:12, NIV)

Wise and Eternal God, I come to You seeking wisdom in managing my time. Help me to number my days and recognize the value of each moment You've given me. Lord, guide me in creating a balanced schedule that allows time for work, family, rest, and spiritual growth. When I feel overwhelmed by the demands on my time, remind me to seek Your guidance and trust in Your perfect timing.

Father, I pray for discipline to avoid time-wasters and distractions that keep me from fulfilling my responsibilities. Teach me to be fully present in each moment, whether I'm working, spending time with family, or resting in Your presence. In Jesus' name, I pray. Amen.

**What time management strategy can you implement
today to better balance your responsibilities?**

Day 66: FIND REST IN GOD'S PRESENCE

"Come to me, all you who are weary and burdened, and I will give you rest"
(Matthew 11:28, NIV)

Loving Savior, I come to You weary and burdened, seeking the rest that only You can provide. In the midst of my busy life, help me to find true rest in Your presence. Teach me to lay my burdens at Your feet and trust in Your care for me and my loved ones.

Lord, show me how to create moments of rest and renewal in my daily life. Help me to prioritize time for prayer, meditation on Your Word, and quiet reflection. When I feel overwhelmed by the demands of work and family, remind me to retreat to Your presence for strength and peace. Amen.

How can you create a restful moment in God's presence today?

*"The wise woman builds her house, but with her
own hands the foolish one tears hers down"*
(Proverbs 14:1, NIV)

Gracious God, grant me wisdom to build a peaceful and nurturing home for my family. Help me to create an environment of love, respect, and spiritual growth. Guide my words and actions to build up my family members rather than tear them down.

Lord, I pray for patience and understanding in my interactions with my family. When conflicts arise, give me the grace to respond with kindness and seek reconciliation. I ask for Your presence to fill our home. May our dwelling be a place of refuge from the stresses of the outside world, where each family member feels valued and supported. In Jesus' name, I pray. Amen.

What specific action can you take today to promote peace in your home?

Day 68: HONOR GOD IN YOUR WORK

*"Whatever you do, work at it with all your heart,
as working for the Lord, not for human masters"*
(Colossians 3:23, NIV)

Lord of All, help me to see my work as an opportunity to honor You. Whether at home or in the workplace, guide me to perform my duties with excellence, integrity, and a positive attitude. Remind me that in all I do, I am ultimately working for You.

Father, when I face challenges or frustrations in my work, give me perseverance and a Christ-like perspective. Help me to be a light in my workplace, demonstrating Your love and grace to my colleagues. Grant me the wisdom to balance my work commitments with my other responsibilities. In Jesus' name, I pray. Amen.

How can you honor God more fully in your work today?

Day 69: NURTURE FAMILY RELATIONSHIPS

"Start children off on the way they should go,
and even when they are old they will not turn from it"
(Proverbs 22:6, NIV)

Heavenly Father, thank You for the gift of family. Guide me in nurturing strong, loving relationships with my family members. Give me wisdom to teach and guide my children in Your ways, setting an example of faith and godly living.

Lord, I pray for patience and understanding in my role as a parent/spouse/family member. Help me to create meaningful moments of connection amidst our busy lives. When conflicts arise, give me the grace to respond with love and seek reconciliation. I ask for Your blessing on our family time together. May our conversations be edifying, our activities be bonding, and our home be filled with Your love. Amen.

What intentional step can you take today to strengthen a family relationship?

Day 70: TRUST GOD WITH YOUR RESPONSIBILITIES

"Cast all your anxiety on him because he cares for you."
(1 Peter 5:7, NIV)

Loving God, I come before You with all my worries and responsibilities. Help me to truly cast my anxieties upon You, trusting in Your care and provision. When I feel overwhelmed by the demands of work and family life, remind me of Your promise to carry my burdens.

Lord, give me the faith to release control and trust in Your perfect plan. When I'm tempted to worry about the future or fret over my to-do list, guide me to turn those concerns into prayers. Grant me the wisdom to steward my time and energy well, and the humility to ask for help when needed. Amen.

What worry do you need to cast upon God today?

Day 71: EMBRACE TRIALS AS OPPORTUNITIES

"Consider it pure joy, my brothers and sisters, whenever you face trials of many kinds"
(James 1:2, NIV)

Heavenly Father, I come before You, acknowledging that trials are a part of life. Help me to see these challenges as opportunities for growth and refinement of my faith. Give me the strength to face trials with joy, knowing that You are working through them for my good.

Lord, when I encounter difficulties, remind me of Your presence and Your promise to never leave me. Help me to trust in Your wisdom and purpose, even when I don't understand the reasons behind my trials. Grant me the perspective to see beyond my immediate circumstances and recognize the potential for spiritual growth. In Jesus' name, I pray. Amen.

How can you reframe a current challenge as an opportunity for spiritual growth?

Day 72: STAND FIRM IN GOD'S STRENGTH

"Be on your guard; stand firm in the faith; be courageous; be strong."
(1 Corinthians 16:13, NIV)

Almighty God, I come to You seeking the strength to stand firm in my faith. Fill me with Your courage and power to face whatever comes my way. When doubts creep in, or opposition arises, remind me of the solid foundation I have in You.

Father, I pray for a bold and steadfast faith that withstands the tests of time and trials. Use the challenges I face to refine my faith and deepen my trust in You. May my unwavering stance be a beacon of hope to others and a testament to Your faithfulness. In Jesus' name, I pray. Amen.

In what area of your life do you need to stand firm in your faith today?

"Not only so, but we also glory in our sufferings,
because we know that suffering produces perseverance"
(Romans 5:3, NIV)

Gracious God, I thank You for the truth that suffering can produce perseverance in my life. Help me to embrace the challenges I face, knowing that they are opportunities to develop endurance and strength of character. Grant me the grace to persevere through difficult times, trusting in Your purpose and plan.

Lord, when I feel weary or discouraged, remind me of the growth that comes through perseverance. Help me to fix my eyes on You and the eternal perspective, rather than focusing solely on my current circumstances. Give me the strength to keep moving forward, even when the path is difficult. In Jesus' name, I pray. Amen.

What challenge are you facing that requires perseverance,
and how can you rely on God's strength to endure?

"For I know the plans I have for you," declares the Lord, "plans to prosper you
and not to harm you, plans to give you hope and a future."
(Jeremiah 29:11, NIV)

Faithful God, I thank You for Your promises that give me hope and assurance for the future. Help me to anchor my faith in Your word, especially when circumstances seem uncertain or challenging. Remind me of Your good plans for my life and Your commitment to my well-being.

Lord, when doubts or fears about the future arise, guide me back to Your promises. Help me to trust in Your perfect timing and Your sovereign control over my life. Grant me the faith to believe in Your goodness, even when I can't see the way forward.

Which of God's promises do you need to hold onto today?

"For God has not given us a spirit of fear, but of power and of love and of a sound mind"
(2 Timothy 1:7, NKJV)

Almighty God, I come before You, acknowledging the fears that sometimes grip my heart. Thank You for the assurance that fear does not come from You, but rather, You give us power, love, and a sound mind. Help me to overcome my fears with faith in Your promises and Your presence.

Lord, when anxious thoughts threaten to overwhelm me, remind me of Your perfect love that casts out all fear. Fill me with Your power to face my challenges courageously. Grant me a sound mind that is focused on Your truth rather than my fears. In Jesus' name, I pray. Amen.

**What fear do you need to surrender to God today,
replacing it with faith in His promises?**

Day 76: LEARN FROM LIFE'S LESSONS

"And we know that in all things God works for the good of those who love him"
(Romans 8:28, NIV)

Wise and Loving God, I thank You for Your promise to work all things for good in my life. Help me to approach every situation, especially the challenging ones, as an opportunity to learn and grow. Grant me the wisdom to discern the lessons You want to teach me through life's experiences.

Lord, when I face difficulties or disappointments, remind me of Your sovereign control over my life. Help me to trust that You are using these experiences to shape me and prepare me for Your purposes. Give me an open and teachable heart, willing to learn from both successes and failures.

What lesson is God teaching you through a challenge in your life?

"He has made everything beautiful in its time."
(Ecclesiastes 3:11, NIV)

Eternal God, I praise You for Your perfect timing in all things. Help me to trust in Your divine schedule, even when things don't happen as quickly or in the way I expect. Give me the patience to wait on Your timing and faith to believe that You are working all things together for good.

Lord, when I feel frustrated by delays or unanswered prayers, remind me of Your wisdom that surpasses my understanding. Help me to surrender my timelines and expectations to You, trusting that Your timing is always perfect. Grant me the grace to use seasons of waiting as opportunities to grow closer to You. Father, I pray for a heart that rests in Your timing. In Jesus' name, I pray. Amen.

In what area of your life do you need to trust God's timing more fully?

Week 12. Seeking Wisdom in Decision Making

Day 78: ASK GOD FOR DISCERNMENT

"If any of you lacks wisdom, you should ask God, who gives generously
to all without finding fault, and it will be given to you"
(James 1:5, NIV)

Heavenly Father, thank You for Your promise to generously give wisdom to those who ask. As I face decisions, both big and small, I ask for Your divine insight and understanding. Lord, when I feel uncertain or confused, remind me to turn to You first. Help me to recognize my own limitations and to rely on Your infinite wisdom.

Father, use the challenges I face to sharpen my spiritual discernment. May the wisdom You provide not only benefit me but also enable me to guide and help others. In Jesus' name, I pray. Amen.

What decision do you need God's wisdom for today?

"Plans fail for lack of counsel, but with many advisers they succeed"
(Proverbs 15:22, NIV)

Wise God, thank You for the gift of community and the wisdom that can be found in godly counsel. Help me to seek out and listen to wise advisers as I navigate important decisions in my life. Grant me discernment to recognize truly godly counsel.

Lord, guard me against pride that might prevent me from seeking advice. Give me a teachable spirit and the humility to consider perspectives different from my own. Help me to build relationships with mature believers who can offer godly wisdom and support. Guide me in weighing advice against Your Word and Your will for my life. May the decisions I make, informed by godly counsel, bring glory to Your name and blessings to others. In Jesus' name, I pray. Amen.

Who are the godly advisers in your life,
and how can you seek their counsel today?

Day 80: TRUST IN GOD'S GUIDANCE

"I will instruct you and teach you in the way you should go;
I will counsel you with my loving eye on you"
(Psalm 32:8, NIV)

Loving Father, I thank You for Your promise to guide and instruct me. Help me to trust in Your direction for my life, knowing that Your loving eye is always upon me. Increase my faith to follow Your leading, even when the path is unclear.

Lord, when I feel lost or unsure of which way to turn, remind me of Your constant presence and guidance. Open my ears to hear Your voice and my eyes to see the way You are directing me. Give me the courage to step out in faith when You call me to move. I pray for a deep sense of peace and assurance as I walk in Your guidance. Amen.

How can you be more attentive to God's guidance in your daily life?

"The simple believe anything, but the prudent give thought to their steps"
(Proverbs 14:15, NIV)

All-knowing God, I come to You seeking prudence and wisdom in making decisions. Help me to carefully weigh my choices, considering their potential consequences and alignment with Your will. Guard me against hasty or ill-considered decisions. When I'm faced with important choices, remind me to take time for thoughtful reflection and prayer.

Father, I pray for a mind that is sharp and discerning and able to critically evaluate the choices I face. Use the decision-making process to deepen my reliance on You and to grow in wisdom. May the careful consideration I give to my choices be a reflection of my desire to honor You in all I do. In Jesus' name, I pray. Amen.

What important decision are you facing that requires careful consideration?

Day 82: ALIGN DECISIONS WITH GOD'S WORD

"Your word is a lamp for my feet, a light on my path"
(Psalm 119:105, NIV)

Gracious God, I thank You for the guidance of Your Word in my life. Help me to align all my decisions with the truth and wisdom found in Scripture. Illuminate my path with the light of Your Word, showing me the way I should go. Lord, when I face difficult choices, direct me to relevant passages in Your Word. Give me an understanding to apply biblical principles to my decision-making process.

Father, I pray for a deep love and reverence for Your Word. Use my study of Scripture to transform my mind and shape my decision-making. In Jesus' name, I pray. Amen.

**How can you incorporate God's Word more
fully into your decision-making process?**

Day 83: CULTIVATE PATIENCE IN DECISION-MAKING

"Wait for the Lord; be strong and take heart and wait for the Lord."
(Psalm 27:14, NIV)

Patient Father, I come to You acknowledging my need for patience in the decision-making process. Help me to resist the urge to rush into decisions and instead wait upon Your timing and guidance. Grant me strength and courage as I wait for Your clear direction.

Lord, when I feel pressured to make quick decisions, remind me of the wisdom that comes from patient consideration. Calm my anxious heart and help me to trust in Your perfect timing. I pray for a spirit of patience that permeates all areas of my life, especially in decision-making. Use the waiting periods to deepen my faith and reliance on You. Amen.

In what area of decision-making do you need to cultivate more patience?

Day 84: TRUST GOD'S SOVEREIGNTY

"In their hearts humans plan their course, but the Lord establishes their steps"
(Proverbs 16:9, NIV)

Sovereign Lord, I praise You for Your ultimate control over all things. Help me to trust in Your sovereignty as I make plans and decisions. Give me the faith to hold my plans loosely, knowing that You are the one who truly establishes my steps.

Lord, when my plans don't unfold as I expect, remind me of Your greater wisdom and purpose. Help me to find peace in surrendering my will to Yours. Grant me the flexibility to adjust my plans as You direct, always trusting in Your perfect guidance. Use the twists and turns in my life's journey to demonstrate Your sovereignty and care. Amen.

**How can you show greater trust in God's sovereignty
in your current circumstances?**

Day 85: UNDERSTAND THE DEPTH OF GOD'S LOVE

*"For God so loved the world that he gave his one and only Son,
that whoever believes in him shall not perish but have eternal life."
(John 3:16, NIV)*

Loving Father, I stand in awe of the depth of Your love for me and for all humanity. Help me to truly grasp the magnitude of Your sacrifice in sending Your Son for our salvation. Open my heart to receive and respond to Your incredible love.

Lord, when I feel unworthy or unloved, remind me of the lengths You went to demonstrate Your love for me. Help me to find my identity and worth in Your love, rather than in the opinions of others or my own accomplishments. Give me the courage to trust in Your love, especially in times of doubt or difficulty. In Jesus' name, I pray. Amen.

How can you demonstrate God's love to someone in your life today?

Day 86: FORGIVENESS THROUGH CHRIST

*"In him we have redemption through his blood, the forgiveness of sins,
in accordance with the riches of God's grace"
(Ephesians 1:7, NIV)*

Merciful God, I thank You for the forgiveness made available through Christ's sacrifice. Help me to fully embrace and appreciate the freedom that comes from being forgiven. Deepen my understanding of the riches of Your grace poured out for me.

Lord, when I struggle with guilt or shame, remind me of the complete forgiveness I have in You. Help me to live in the reality of being redeemed and forgiven, letting go of past mistakes, and embracing the new life You offer. Give me the strength to forgive others as You have forgiven me.

**Is there an area in your life where you need to
more fully embrace God's forgiveness?**

*"For the message of the cross is foolishness to those who are perishing,
but to us who are being saved it is the power of God."*
(1 Corinthians 1:18, NIV)

Almighty God, I come before You in awe of the power of the cross. Help me to fully recognize and embrace the transformative power of Christ's sacrifice in my life. Open my eyes to see the cross not as foolishness, but as the ultimate demonstration of Your power and love.

Lord, when the world mocks or dismisses the message of the cross, give me the courage to stand firm in my faith. Help me to experience the power of the cross in overcoming sin, fear, and death in my own life. Grant me wisdom to apply the truths of the cross to my daily challenges and decisions. Amen.

How has the power of the cross been evident in your life recently?

Day 88: FREEDOM THROUGH CHRIST'S SACRIFICE

*"It is for freedom that Christ has set us free. Stand firm, then,
and do not let yourselves be burdened again by a yoke of slavery."*
(Galatians 5:1, NIV)

Liberating God, I thank You for the freedom Christ has won for me through His sacrifice. Help me to fully embrace and live in this freedom, resisting the temptation to return to old patterns of bondage. Give me the strength to stand firm in the liberty You have provided.

Lord, when I feel tempted to fall back into legalism or sin, remind me of the price paid for my freedom. Help me to walk in the freedom of Your grace, living not in fear but in the confident assurance of Your love and acceptance. Grant me discernment to recognize and reject anything that would enslave me again. Amen.

**In what area of your life do you need to more fully e
mbrace the freedom Christ has won for you?**

Day 89: EMBRACE NEW LIFE IN CHRIST

"Therefore, if anyone is in Christ, the new creation has come:
The old has gone, the new is here!"
(2 Corinthians 5:17, NIV)

Creator God, I praise You for the new life You offer in Christ. Help me to fully embrace my identity as a new creation, leaving behind the old ways and walking confidently in the new life You have given me. Renew my mind and transform my heart to align with Your will.

Lord, when I struggle with old habits or thought patterns, remind me of the new nature You have given me. Help me to put off the old self and put on the new, living each day in the reality of being a new creation in Christ. Give me the courage to embrace the changes You are working on in my life. May the evidence of new life would be visible in my attitudes, actions, and relationships. Amen.

What aspect of your new life in Christ do you need to more fully embrace today?

Day 90: SHARE THE MESSAGE OF SALVATION

"For I am not ashamed of the gospel, because it is the power
of God that brings salvation to everyone who believes"
(Romans 1:16, NIV)

Gracious God, I thank You for the powerful message of salvation through Christ. Give me the boldness to share this good news with others, never being ashamed of the gospel. Help me to trust in the power of Your message to transform lives.

Lord, when I feel inadequate or afraid to share my faith, remind me that it is Your power, not my eloquence, that brings salvation. Help me to clearly and compassionately communicate the hope I have in Christ. Grant me wisdom to recognize opportunities to share the gospel and the courage to act on them. Please use me as an instrument of Your salvation in the lives of others. Amen.

With whom can you share the message of salvation this week?

Day 91: REFLECT ON CHRIST'S HUMILITY

*"And being found in appearance as a man, he humbled himself
by becoming obedient to death—even death on a cross!"*
(Philippians 2:8, NIV)

Humble Savior, I stand in awe of Your willingness to lay aside Your glory and humble Yourself for our sake. Help me to truly comprehend the depth of Your humility in becoming human and submitting to death on a cross. Let Your example transform my heart and actions.

Lord, when pride or self-importance creep into my life, remind me of Your ultimate act of humility. Help me to follow Your example, considering others above myself and being willing to serve even when it's costly or uncomfortable. Grant me the strength to be obedient to Your will, even when it requires personal sacrifice. Amen.

In what specific way can you practice Christ-like humility today?

April

Week 14. Embracing Hope and New Beginnings

Day 92: CELEBRATE THE RESURRECTION

*"Praise be to the God and Father of our Lord Jesus Christ! In his great
mercy he has given us new birth into a living hope through
the resurrection of Jesus Christ from the dead"*
(1 Peter 1:3, NIV)

Risen Lord, I come before You with a heart full of praise for the miracle of Your resurrection. Thank You for the living hope You've given me through Your victory over death. Help me to live each day in the power and joy of Your resurrection.

Father, when doubts or discouragement threaten to overwhelm me, remind me of the empty tomb and the new life it represents. Fill me with the assurance that comes from knowing You have conquered sin and death. Grant me the courage to face life's challenges with resurrection faith. Amen,

How can you share the hope of the resurrection today?

Day 93: EMBRACE GOD'S RENEWAL

"See, I am doing a new thing! Now it springs up; do you not perceive it?"
(Isaiah 43:19, NIV)

Creator God, I thank You for Your promise of renewal and new beginnings. Open my eyes to see the new things You are doing in my life and in the world around me. Give me the faith to embrace Your plans for renewal, even when they challenge my expectations.

Lord, when I feel stuck in old patterns or discouraged by past failures, remind me of Your power to make all things new. Help me to let go of what lies behind and to reach forward to what lies ahead. Grant me the courage to step into the new opportunities You are creating for me. Father, I pray that I will be an active participant in Your work of renewal. Amen.

**What area of your life needs God's renewal,
and how can you cooperate with His work?**

Day 94: WALK IN NEWNESS OF LIFE

*"We were therefore buried with him through baptism into death in order that,
just as Christ was raised from the dead through the glory of the Father,
we too may live a new life"*
(Romans 6:4, NIV)

Gracious Father, I thank You for the new life You've given me through Christ's death and resurrection. Help me to fully embrace and live out this new life, dying to sin and living for righteousness. Guide me in walking daily in the newness of life. You've provided.

Lord, when I'm tempted to fall back into old patterns of sin, remind me of my identity in Christ and the new life I now have. Empower me by Your Spirit to put off the old self and put on the new, living in a way that reflects Your character and values. Grant me wisdom to make choices that align with my new life in Christ. Amen.

How can you demonstrate your new life in Christ today?

*"Because of the Lord's great love we are not consumed, for his compassions
never fail. They are new every morning; great is your faithfulness"
(Lamentations 3:22–23, NIV)*

Faithful God, I praise You for Your unfailing love and compassion that are new every morning. Help me to anchor my hope in Your unchanging faithfulness, especially during times of uncertainty or difficulty. Remind me daily of Your steadfast love that never ceases.

Lord, when I feel overwhelmed or discouraged, turn my focus to Your faithfulness. Help me to see each new day as a fresh opportunity to experience Your compassion and grace. Grant me the faith to trust in Your goodness, even when circumstances seem bleak. Use my confidence in Your steadfast love to encourage others who may be struggling to find hope. Amen.

How can you remind yourself of God's faithfulness throughout your day?

Day 96: EMBRACE YOUR IDENTITY IN CHRIST

*"Therefore, if anyone is in Christ, the new creation has come:
The old has gone, the new is here!"
(2 Corinthians 5:17, NIV)*

Loving Father, I thank You for making me a new creation in Christ. Help me to fully embrace my new identity, leaving behind the old self and living in the reality of who I am in You. Renew my mind daily with the truth of Your Word about who You say I am.

Lord, when I struggle with old insecurities or past mistakes, remind me of the new identity You've given me. Help me to see myself through Your eyes, as Your beloved child and a new creation. Grant me the courage to live out this new identity in my relationships and daily choices. May my life reflect the reality of being a new creation. In Jesus' name, I pray. Amen.

What aspect of your identity in Christ do you need to more fully embrace today?

*"May the God of hope fill you with all joy and peace as you trust in him,
so that you may overflow with hope by the power of the Holy Spirit."
(Romans 15:13, NIV)*

God of Hope, I come before You, asking to be filled with Your joy and peace. Increase my trust in You so that I may overflow with hope through the power of Your Holy Spirit. Help me to cultivate a spirit of hope that remains steadfast even in challenging times.

Lord, when circumstances tempt me to despair, remind me of the unshakeable hope I have in You. Help me to focus on Your promises and Your faithfulness rather than on the problems around me. Grant me the strength to be a bearer of hope to those who are struggling. Please produce in me a deep, abiding hope that is contagious to those around me. In Jesus' name, I pray. Amen.

How can you cultivate and share hope with someone in your life today?

*"For the wages of sin is death, but the gift of God is eternal life in Christ Jesus our Lord"
(Romans 6:23, NIV)*

Eternal God, I thank You for the incredible gift of eternal life through Jesus Christ. Help me to live with an eternal perspective, valuing the things that have lasting significance. Increase my appreciation for the free gift of salvation and the promise of eternity with You. Help me to make choices that reflect my citizenship in heaven and my hope for eternity.

Father, I pray that the reality of eternal life would shape my priorities and motivate my service to You and others. Use my eternal perspective to challenge those around me to consider their own eternal destiny. Amen.

How can you live today with an eternal perspective?

Day 99: CHOOSE JOY IN ALL CIRCUMSTANCES

"Rejoice always"
(1 Thessalonians 5:16, NIV)

Joyful Father, I thank You for the command to rejoice always. Help me to choose joy in all circumstances, recognizing that true joy comes from You and not from my situation. Give me the strength to rejoice even in difficult times, knowing that You are with me.

Lord, when I face challenges or disappointments, remind me of the reasons I have to rejoice in You. Help me to focus on Your goodness, love, and faithfulness rather than on my problems. Grant me the perspective to see beyond my current circumstances and find joy in Your eternal promises. Amen.

How can you choose joy in the challenging situation you're facing today?

Day 100: GUARD YOUR THOUGHTS

"Finally, brothers and sisters, whatever is true, whatever is noble, whatever is right, whatever is pure, whatever is lovely, whatever is admirable—if anything is excellent or praiseworthy—think about such things"
(Philippians 4:8, NIV)

Righteous God, I thank You for the guidance You provide for our thought life. Help me to guard my mind and focus on things that are pleasing to You. Give me discernment to recognize thoughts that are not aligned with Your will and the strength to replace them with godly thoughts.

Lord, when negative or impure thoughts threaten to take hold, remind me of this verse and guide me to refocus my mind on what is true, noble, right, pure, lovely, and admirable. Amen.

What specific thoughts do you need to replace with more godly ones today?

"The tongue has the power of life and death, and those who love it will eat its fruit"
(Proverbs 18:21, NIV)

Gracious God, I thank You for the gift of speech and the power of words. Help me to use my tongue wisely, speaking words that bring life, encouragement, and healing to others. Give me the self-control to refrain from harmful speech and the wisdom to choose words that build up rather than tear down.

Lord, when I'm tempted to speak carelessly or unkindly, remind me of the impact my words can have. Help me to think before I speak, considering whether my words align with Your love and truth. Grant me the courage to speak words of life, even in difficult conversations or conflicts. May my words be a source of blessing, comfort, and inspiration to those around me. In Jesus' name, I pray. Amen.

How can you intentionally speak words of life to someone today?

Day 102: CULTIVATE GRATITUDE

"Give thanks in all circumstances; for this is God's will for you in Christ Jesus"
(1 Thessalonians 5:18, NIV)

Generous Father, I thank You for Your command to cultivate gratitude in all circumstances. Help me to develop a heart of thankfulness, recognizing Your blessings even in challenging times. Give me the faith to trust that You are working for my good in every situation.

Lord, when I'm tempted to complain or focus on what I lack, remind me of the many reasons I have to be grateful. Help me to see Your hand at work in all aspects of my life, acknowledging Your provision, protection, and presence. Grant me the perspective to find reasons for thanksgiving, even in difficult circumstances.

What are three things you can thank God for right now,
especially in challenging circumstances?

*"And we know that in all things God works for the good of those
who love him, who have been called according to his purpose"*
(Romans 8:28, NIV)

Faithful God, I thank You for Your promise to work all things for good in the lives of those who love You. Help me to trust in Your goodness, especially when circumstances are difficult or confusing. Increase my faith to believe that You are always working for my ultimate good and Your glory.

Help me to see beyond my immediate circumstances and trust in Your bigger plan. Grant me patience to wait for Your good purposes to unfold, even when I can't see or understand them at the moment. Deepen my trust in God's goodness. Use my confidence in Your good plans as a witness to others who may be struggling to see Your hand at work. In Jesus' name, I pray. Amen.

**How can you demonstrate trust in God's goodness
in a current challenging situation?**

Day 104: EMBRACE HOPE FOR THE FUTURE

*"For I know the plans I have for you," declares the Lord, "plans to prosper
you and not to harm you, plans to give you hope and a future."*
(Jeremiah 29:11, NIV)

God of Hope, I thank You for Your promise of a hopeful future. Help me to embrace the plans You have for me, trusting that they are good and purposeful. Give me the faith to look forward with excitement and confidence, knowing that You hold my future in Your hands.

Lord, when I feel uncertain or anxious about what lies ahead, remind me of Your loving intentions for my life. Help me to release my own plans and expectations, surrendering to Your perfect will. Grant me the courage to step into the future You have prepared, even when it requires leaving my comfort zone. Amen.

How can you actively embrace hope for your future today?

"A new command I give you: Love one another.
As I have loved you, so you must love one another"
(John 13:34, NIV)

Loving Father, I thank You for the perfect example of love You've given us in Jesus. Help me to obey Your command to love others as You have loved me. Fill me with Your love so that it overflows to those around me, reflecting Your character and drawing others to You.

Lord, when loving others is challenging, remind me of the sacrificial love You've shown me. Help me to extend grace, forgiveness, and compassion to others, even when it's difficult. Grant me the strength to love selflessly and unconditionally, putting others' needs before my own. Use my words, actions, and attitudes to demonstrate Your love to everyone I encounter. In Jesus' name, I pray. Amen.

In what specific way can you show God's love to someone today?

Week 16. Praying for Our Nation

Day 106: GOD'S GUIDANCE FOR THE COUNTRY

"Blessed is the nation whose God is the Lord, the people he chose for his inheritance"
(Psalm 33:12, NIV)

Sovereign Lord, I come before You seeking Your guidance for our nation. Help us as a country to acknowledge You as our God and to follow Your ways. May we recognize our need for Your wisdom and direction in all aspects of our national life.

Father, when our nation strays from Your paths, remind us of the blessings that come from honoring You. Guide our leaders, institutions, and citizens to seek Your will in decision-making and policy-forming. Grant us the humility to turn to You for guidance in times of national crisis and prosperity alike.

How can you actively seek God's guidance for your nation today?

"I urge, then, first of all, that petitions, prayers, intercession and thanksgiving
be made for all people—for kings and all those in authority"
(1 Timothy 2:1-2, NIV)

Almighty God, I lift up our national leaders to You. Grant them wisdom, integrity, and compassion as they govern our country. Help them to lead with justice, to seek the welfare of all citizens, and to make decisions that honor You.

Lord, when our leaders face difficult challenges, guide them to seek Your counsel. Protect them from corruption and self-interest, and help them to prioritize the good of the nation over personal gain. Give them the courage to stand for what is right, even when it's unpopular. Today, I pray for a spiritual awakening among our national leaders. Amen.

How can you commit to regularly praying for your national leaders?

Day 108: INTERCEDE FOR JUSTICE

"Righteousness exalts a nation, but sin condemns any people."
(Proverbs 14:34, NIV)

Righteous God, I intercede for our nation, asking that justice and righteousness would prevail in our land. Help us as a society to value and pursue what is right in Your eyes. Convict us of our national sins and lead us to repentance.

Lord, when injustice and unrighteousness seem to dominate, remind us of Your call to be salt and light in our world. Guide our nation's laws, policies, and cultural values to align with Your standards of justice and righteousness. Grant courage to those who stand for what is right in the face of opposition. I pray for a movement of righteousness to sweep across our nation. Amen.

What specific area of injustice in your nation
can you pray about and act on today?

"If my people, who are called by my name, will humble themselves and pray and seek my face and turn from their wicked ways, then I will hear from heaven, and I will forgive their sin and will heal their land."
(2 Chronicles 7:14, NIV)

Healing God, I come before You on behalf of our nation, asking for Your forgiveness and healing. Help us as Your people to humble ourselves, to pray fervently, to seek Your face wholeheartedly, and to turn from our wicked ways. Bring conviction of sin and a spirit of repentance to our land.

Lord, when we see the brokenness in our nation, remind us of Your promise to heal our land if we turn to You. Guide us in identifying and confronting the sins that have taken root in our society. May our nation experience Your forgiveness and healing. In Jesus' name, I pray. Amen.

How can you participate in seeking God's healing for your nation?

Day 110: SEEK PEACE FOR THE NATION

"Also, seek the peace and prosperity of the city to which I have carried you into exile. Pray to the Lord for it, because if it prospers, you too will prosper"
(Jeremiah 29:7, NIV)

Prince of Peace, I come before You, seeking peace and prosperity for our nation. Guide us as a society to pursue harmony, understanding, and mutual respect among all people. Help us to work together for the common good and the flourishing of our country.

Lord, when division and conflict threaten our national unity, remind us of our call to be peacemakers. Guide our leaders and citizens in finding peaceful resolutions to disagreements and in bridging divides. Grant wisdom in addressing the root causes of unrest and instability in our nation. Amen.

**What specific prayer can you offer for a current
conflict or division in your nation?**

"How good and pleasant it is when God's people live together in unity!"
(Psalm 133:1, NIV)

God of Unity, I lift up our nation to You, asking for a spirit of unity to prevail among our people. Help us to overcome divisions of race, politics, and social status, recognizing our shared humanity and citizenship. Guide us in finding common ground and working together for the good of all.

Lord, when polarization and discord threaten to tear us apart, remind us of the beauty and strength found in unity. Help us to listen to one another with empathy and respect, seeking understanding even in our differences. Grant our leaders wisdom in fostering a sense of national unity and shared purpose. Holy Spirit, I pray for a renewed sense of national identity and cohesion. Amen.

How can you actively promote unity in your sphere of influence today?

Day 112: INTERCEDE FOR SPIRITUAL AWAKENING

"Restore us, Lord God Almighty; make your face shine on us, that we may be saved"
(Psalm 80:19, NIV)

Almighty God, I intercede for our nation, asking for a widespread spiritual awakening. Revive Your church and draw multitudes to saving faith in Jesus Christ. Let Your face shine upon us, bringing restoration and salvation to our land.

Lord, when spiritual apathy or darkness seems to prevail, remind us of Your power to bring revival and transformation. Spark a hunger for You in the hearts of our people. Grant boldness to Your church in proclaiming the gospel and demonstrating Your love to our nation. Amen.

How can you contribute to spiritual awakening in your community and nation?

Day 113: CULTIVATE MUTUAL RESPECT

"Submit to one another out of reverence for Christ."
(Ephesians 5:21, NIV)

Heavenly Father, I thank You for the gift of marriage. Help us to cultivate mutual respect, submitting to one another out of reverence for Christ. Teach us to value each other's thoughts, feelings, and contributions.

Lord, when pride or selfishness threatens our unity, remind us of Your call to mutual submission. Help us to put each other's needs before our own, following Christ's example of selfless love. Grant us the humility to listen, understand, and honor one another. May our relationship reflect Your design for partnerships, characterized by love, respect, and unity. In Jesus' name, I pray. Amen.

How can you show greater respect to your spouse today?

Day 114: NURTURE LOVE AND AFFECTION

"Above all, love each other deeply, because love covers over a multitude of sins"
(1 Peter 4:8, NIV)

Gracious God, I thank You for the love You've given us for one another. Help us to nurture and deepen that love, covering each other's faults with grace and forgiveness. Teach us to express our affection freely and sincerely.

Lord, when the pressures of life threaten to dampen our love, remind us of its importance above all else. Help us to prioritize our relationship, making time to cultivate intimacy and affection. Grant us creativity in expressing our love in ways that are meaningful to our spouse. In Jesus' name, I pray. Amen.

What specific act of love can you show your spouse today?

"Bear with each other and forgive one another if any of you has a grievance against someone. Forgive as the Lord forgave you"
(Colossians 3:13, NIV)

Merciful Father, I thank You for Your forgiveness towards us. Help us to extend that same forgiveness to each other in our marriage. Teach us to bear with one another's faults and to release grievances quickly. When hurt or resentment builds up, remind us of the forgiveness we've received from You. Help us to let go of past offenses and to choose reconciliation over holding grudges.

Holy Spirit, grant us the strength to forgive even when it's difficult. Cultivate a spirit of forgiveness in our relationship. Use our willingness to forgive as a means of healing and strengthening our bond. In Jesus' name, I pray. Amen.

Is there something you need to forgive your spouse for today?

Day 116: COMMUNICATE WITH GRACE

"Let your conversation be always full of grace, seasoned with salt, so that you may know how to answer everyone"
(Colossians 4:6, NIV)

Wise God, I thank You for the gift of communication. Help us to speak to each other with grace and wisdom, seasoning our words with kindness and truth. Teach us to listen actively and respond thoughtfully.

Lord, when misunderstandings or conflicts arise, remind us of the power of gracious communication. Help us to choose our words carefully, speaking the truth in love. Grant us patience in listening and wisdom in responding, especially during difficult conversations. May our communication be a source of encouragement and growth in our relationship. In Jesus' name, I pray. Amen.

How can you communicate more graciously with your spouse today?

"Therefore what God has joined together, let no one separate."
(Mark 10:9, NIV)

Heavenly Father, I come before You with a heart overflowing with gratitude for the sacred bond of marriage, a gift that enriches my life in countless ways. Thank You for the love, companionship, and partnership I am privileged to share with my spouse, and for the journey we embark on together each day. I ask for Your wisdom to guide me and Your strength to fortify my commitment, ensuring that my vows remain a constant testament to my enduring love and dedication.

Lord, when we face trials that challenge our unity, remind us of the divine nature of our union. Empower us with the courage to confront obstacles together, leaning on Your eternal strength to uphold and sustain us. May our marriage be a reflection of Your endless love and grace. Amen.

How can you reaffirm your commitment to your spouse today?

Day 118: SERVE ONE ANOTHER

"Serve one another humbly in love."
(Galatians 5:13, NIV)

Servant King, I thank You for modeling selfless service. Help us to serve one another humbly in our marriage, putting each other's needs before our own. Teach us to find joy in caring for and supporting our spouse. Help us to notice and respond to our spouse's needs, both spoken and unspoken.

Grant us creativity and enthusiasm in finding ways to serve and bless each other daily. Use our acts of service to strengthen our bond and demonstrate our love tangibly. May our mutual service create an atmosphere of love, appreciation, and support in our relationship. In Jesus' name, I pray. Amen.

What specific act of service can you do for your spouse today?

"For where two or three gather in my name, there am I with them"
(Matthew 18:20, NIV)

Heavenly Father, I thank You for the privilege of prayer. Help us to make praying together a priority in our marriage, inviting Your presence and guidance into our partnership. Teach us to share our hearts with You and each other through prayer.

Holy Spirit, I pray that You would deepen our spiritual intimacy through shared prayer. Use our time of prayer to align our hearts with each other and with You. May our practice of praying together strengthen our relationship, guide our decisions, and be a source of comfort and unity in all circumstances. In Jesus' name, I pray. Amen.

How can you initiate or enhance your practice
of praying together with your spouse?

May

Week 18. Honoring Motherhood

Day 120: EMBRACE THE GIFT OF MOTHERHOOD

"Children are a heritage from the Lord, offspring a reward from him"
(Psalm 127:3, NIV)

Gracious Father, what a precious gift You've entrusted to me in motherhood. In moments of joy and challenge, help me remember that my children are Your heritage, a divine reward. Let this truth sink deep into my heart, coloring every interaction with my little ones. Grant me eyes to see beyond the mundane tasks to the sacred work of nurturing these young lives.

Lord, may I steward this gift with reverence and joy, always mindful of Your presence in our family life. Fill me with wonder at the miracle of life and growth unfolding before me. Amen.

How can you celebrate the gift of motherhood in a special way today?

"Start children off on the way they should go,
and even when they are old they will not turn from it"
(Proverbs 22:6, NIV)

Wise Counselor, I stand in awe of the responsibility You've given me to guide these young hearts. Pour out Your wisdom upon me as I navigate the complex journey of parenthood. In moments of uncertainty, be my steady compass. When I lack answers, be my source of insight. Grant me the humility to learn from others and the courage to follow Your leading, even when it differs from worldly advice.

May the seeds of truth and love I plant today bear fruit in my children's lives for years to come. Guide my words, actions, and decisions to align with Your perfect will for their lives. Amen.

What area of parenting do you most need God's wisdom for right now?

Day 122: FIND STRENGTH IN GOD'S GRACE

"But he said to me, 'My grace is sufficient for you,
for my power is made perfect in weakness'"
(2 Corinthians 12:9, NIV)

Lord of Strength, in my weakness as a mother, I turn to You. Your grace is my lifeline in moments of exhaustion, doubt, and overwhelm. Help me embrace my limitations, knowing that they create space for Your power to shine through. Use my struggles as opportunities to demonstrate dependence on You, teaching my little ones the beauty of relying on Your strength.

Thank You for Your endless supply of grace that meets me in every challenging moment of motherhood. May I be a channel of that grace to my family and others around me. Amen.

How can you lean into God's grace in a challenging area of motherhood today?

"Love is patient, love is kind. It does not envy, it does not boast, it is not proud"
(1 Corinthians 13:4, NIV)

Loving Father, mold my heart to reflect Your patient, kind love in my role as a mother. When frustrations mount, and patience wears thin, infuse me with Your supernatural love that endures all things. Teach me to love my children with a love that is not easily angered and keeps no record of wrongs.

Help me set aside my own agenda and pride to truly see and meet their needs. May my love create a safe haven where they can grow, make mistakes, and learn without fear of judgment. Lord, let Your love flow through me, nurturing my children's hearts and pointing them towards You, the source of perfect love. Amen.

**In what situation with your children do you need
to show more patience and kindness today?**

Day 124: MODEL FAITH FOR YOUR CHILDREN

*"Only be careful, and watch yourselves closely so that you do not forget the
things your eyes have seen or let them fade from your heart as long as you live.
Teach them to your children and to their children after them"*
(Deuteronomy 4:9, NIV)

Faithful God, impress upon my heart the weight of modeling faith for my children. Help me live out my beliefs authentically, letting them see Your work in my life. Give me eyes to recognize teachable moments and the wisdom to share Your truths in ways they can understand.

Lord, guard my heart against the forgetfulness of Your mighty deeds. Keep Your Word and Your works fresh in my mind, that I might pass them on to the next generation. Amen.

**What aspect of your faith can you intentionally
model or discuss with your children today?**

Day 125: BALANCE ROLES WITH GRACE

"She watches over the affairs of her household and does not eat the bread of idleness"
(Proverbs 31:27, NIV)

Master Orchestrator, grant me wisdom to balance the many roles You've entrusted to me. As I juggle the responsibilities of motherhood with other callings, help me prioritize according to Your will. Give me discernment to know when to work and when to rest.

Lord, infuse my efforts with purpose and diligence. Guard me against both laziness and the trap of busyness for its own sake. Help me create a home atmosphere that nurtures both productivity and peace, reflecting Your perfect balance of work and rest. Grant me the strength to faithfully steward all You've given me, trusting You to multiply my efforts for Your glory. Amen.

How can you bring more intentionality and balance to your various roles today?

Day 126: TRUST GOD WITH YOUR CHILDREN

"For I know the plans I have for you,' declares the Lord, 'plans to prosper
you and not to harm you, plans to give you hope and a future'"
(Jeremiah 29:11, NIV)

Sovereign Lord, I entrust my precious children into Your capable hands. Remind me that You love them even more than I do, and that Your plans for them are perfect. Help me release my grip on their lives, allowing You to work out Your purposes in Your timing.

Give me faith to believe that You are actively working for their good, even when circumstances seem challenging. Use me as an instrument in Your plan for my children's lives, but help me always point them to You as the author of their story. Amen.

In what area do you need to trust God more fully with your children's lives?

Day 127: EMBRACE SPIRITUAL FREEDOM

"It is for freedom that Christ has set us free. Stand firm, then,
and do not let yourselves be burdened again by a yoke of slavery."
(Galatians 5:1, NIV)

Liberating God, how profound is the freedom You've granted us through Christ! Today, I choose to embrace this spiritual liberty fully. Break any chains of legalism, guilt, or fear that still bind me. Help me stand firm in the freedom You've won, resisting any attempt of the enemy to re-enslave my soul.

Lord, when old habits or thoughts threaten to burden me, remind me of the price paid for my freedom. May I live each moment in the joyous reality of being Your free child, unencumbered by the weight of sin and shame. Amen.

How can you more fully embrace and live out your spiritual freedom today?

Day 128: LIVE IN THE FREEDOM OF FORGIVENESS

"In him we have redemption through his blood, the forgiveness of sins,
in accordance with the riches of God's grace"
(Ephesians 1:7, NIV)

Merciful Father, what a gift You've given us in the freedom of forgiveness! Today, I bask in the wonder of being fully forgiven through Christ's sacrifice. Help me grasp the depth of this truth, letting it permeate every aspect of my being.

Lord, please help me to live unburdened by past mistakes. Let the reality of Your forgiveness free me to forgive others generously, breaking cycles of bitterness and resentment. Amen.

How can you extend the freedom of forgiveness to someone in your life today?

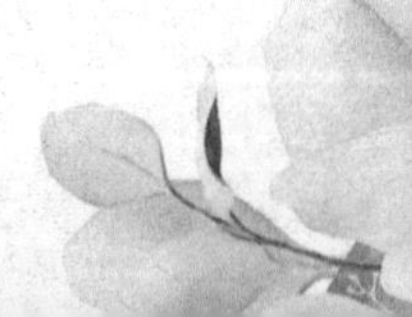

"You, my brothers and sisters, were called to be free. But do not use your freedom to indulge the flesh; rather, serve one another humbly in love"
(Galatians 5:13, NIV)

Selfless Savior, thank You for the freedom You've given me. Today, help me use this liberty not for my own indulgence, but as an opportunity to serve others in love. Show me how to channel my freedom into acts of kindness and compassion.

Lord, when I'm tempted to use my freedom selfishly, redirect my focus to the needs of those around me. May my life demonstrate that true freedom is found in giving, not taking. Grant me creativity and enthusiasm in finding ways to serve, seeing each opportunity as a chance to reflect Your love. Let my service be a powerful testimony to the liberating and transforming power of Your love. Amen.

**What specific act of service can you do today
as an expression of your freedom in Christ?**

Day 130: STAND FIRM IN LIBERTY

"Now the Lord is the Spirit, and where the Spirit of the Lord is, there is freedom"
(2 Corinthians 3:17, NIV)

Spirit of the Living God, I rejoice in the freedom that comes from Your presence in my life. Today, help me stand firm in this liberty, resisting any attempt of the enemy to rob me of the freedom You've given. May Your presence be so evident in my life that others are drawn to the freedom found in You.

Remind me that true freedom is not dependent on external factors but on Your indwelling Spirit. Help me to cultivate an awareness of Your presence throughout my day, knowing that where You are, freedom flourishes. Amen.

How can you cultivate a greater awareness of God's presence?

*"For the Spirit God gave us does not make us timid,
but gives us power, love and self-discipline"
(2 Timothy 1:7, NIV)*

Mighty God, I come to You, asking for freedom from fear. Replace my timidity with the power, love, and self-discipline that come from Your Spirit. Help me break free from the paralyzing grip of fear and step boldly into the life You've called me to live.

When anxious thoughts threaten to overwhelm me, remind me of the spirit of courage You've placed within me. May Your perfect love cast out all fear, freeing me to live and love boldly. Grant me the self-discipline to focus on Your truths rather than my fears. Lord, use the process of overcoming fear in my life as a testimony to Your power. Amen.

What specific fear do you need to confront and overcome with God's help today?

Day 132: EMBRACE FREEDOM FROM SIN

*"But now that you have been set free from sin and have become slaves of God,
the benefit you reap leads to holiness, and the result is eternal life"
(Romans 6:22, NIV)*

Holy God, I thank You for setting me free from the power of sin. Today, help me fully embrace this freedom, living as Your devoted servant rather than a slave to my old nature. May I continually choose holiness, delighting in the new life You've given me.

Lord, when temptation arises, remind me of my new identity in You. Help me see that true freedom is found not in indulging my desires, but in aligning my will with Yours. Grant me strength to resist sin and pursue righteousness, knowing that this path leads to life. Continue Your sanctifying work in me. Amen.

What sins make you forget that you're truly free from its bondage?

"So if the Son sets you free, you will be free indeed."
(John 8:36, NIV)

Heavenly Father, what a privilege to be called Your child and to experience the freedom that comes with this identity! Today, help me live fully in the reality of being Your free and beloved child. May every thought, word, and action flow from this foundational truth.

Lord Jesus, thank You for the freedom You won for me. When doubts or insecurities arise, remind me of the completeness of the liberty You provide. Help me to walk in confidence, knowing that I am truly free indeed because of Your work in my life. May I live each moment in joyful awareness of my status as Your free child. Amen.

**How can you more fully embrace and express
your identity as God's free child today?**

Week 20. Finding Rest and Renewal

Day 134: EMBRACE GOD'S INVITATION TO REST

"Come to me, all you who are weary and burdened, and I will give you rest"
(Matthew 11:28, NIV)

Loving Father, I hear Your invitation to rest, and I come to You with all my weariness and burdens. The weight of responsibilities, worries, and expectations has left me exhausted. I long for the deep, soul-refreshing rest that only You can provide. Help me to fully release my cares into Your capable hands, trusting that You will carry what I cannot.

As I enter into Your rest, renew my strength and restore my joy. May this time of rest not only rejuvenate my body, but also deepen my relationship with You. Thank You for Your promise of rest and for Your constant care for me. In Jesus' name, Amen.

How can you practically respond to God's invitation to rest today?

"The Lord is my shepherd, I lack nothing. He makes me lie down in green pastures, he leads me beside quiet waters, he refreshes my soul."
(Psalm 23:1-3, NIV)

Heavenly Shepherd, I thank You for Your faithful provision in my life. Like a caring shepherd, You lead me to places of abundance and peace. Help me to trust fully in Your provision, especially in times when resources seem scarce or the future uncertain.

Lord, refresh my soul with the assurance of Your care. When worry about provision creeps in, guide me back to the quiet waters of Your peace. Help me to be content in all circumstances. Remind me that in You, I truly lack nothing. In Jesus' name, Amen.

In what area of your life do you need to trust God's provision more fully?

Day 136: FIND PEACE IN GOD'S PRESENCE

"You will keep in perfect peace those whose minds are steadfast, because they trust in you"
(Isaiah 26:3, NIV)

Prince of Peace, in the midst of life's chaos and uncertainties, I come seeking the perfect peace that only You can provide. When my mind is filled with worries and my heart with fears, help me to focus steadfastly on You. Quiet the noise in my mind with the assurance of Your presence.

Lord, let Your peace guard my heart and mind in Christ Jesus. As I experience Your perfect peace, help me to be a calming presence to those around me. Thank You for the promise of Your peace that surpasses all understanding. In Jesus' name, Amen.

What specific steps can you take to maintain a steadfast mind focused on God amidst life's challenges?

"But those who hope in the Lord will renew their strength. They will soar on wings like eagles; they will run and not grow weary, they will walk and not be faint"
(Isaiah 40:31, NIV)

Almighty God, I come to You feeling weak and weary. The challenges of life have drained my strength, and I need Your divine renewal. I place my hope fully in You, trusting that You will replenish my depleted resources. Lift me up on wings like eagles, giving me a new perspective on my circumstances.

Lord, as You renew my strength, help me to use it in service to You and others. May the energy and vitality You provide be a testimony to Your power working in me. In Jesus' name, Amen.

How can you apply the concept of "waiting on the Lord"
to a current situation in your life?

Day 138: PRACTICE SABBATH REST

"There remains, then, a Sabbath-rest for the people of God."
(Hebrews 4:9, NIV)

Heavenly Father, thank You for the gift of Sabbath rest. In a world that never stops, help me to pause and enter into the rest You provide. Guide me in setting aside time to cease from my labors, to quiet my mind, and to focus on You. May this practice of Sabbath refresh my soul, realign my priorities, and deepen my trust in Your provision.

Lord, as I rest in You, renew my perspective on work and productivity. Help me to find the balance between diligent labor and restful trust in Your care. Use this time of rest to strengthen my relationships with You and with others. In Jesus' name, Amen.

What changes can you make to your routine to
incorporate more meaningful Sabbath rest?

"Refresh my heart in Christ."
(Philemon 1:20, NIV)

Gracious God, I come to Your Word seeking refreshment for my weary heart. As I read and meditate on Scripture, may it be like a cool drink to my parched soul, nourishing food for my hungry spirit, and a soothing balm for my wounded heart. Open my eyes to see new depths in Your Word, and give me wisdom to apply its truths to my life.

Lord, let Your Word wash over me, cleansing away doubts and renewing my mind. Strengthen my faith through the promises in Scripture and guide my steps by its wisdom. As I find refreshment in Your Word, help me to share its life-giving message with others. May the joy and peace I find in Your Word overflow into my interactions, bringing refreshment to those around me. Amen.

Which passage of Scripture do you find most refreshing,
and how can you engage with it more deeply?

Day 140: EMBRACE SPIRITUAL RENEWAL

"Therefore we do not lose heart. Though outwardly we are wasting away,
yet inwardly we are being renewed day by day"
(2 Corinthians 4:16, NIV)

Heavenly Father, I come before You, aware of my need for spiritual renewal. Though I may feel the effects of aging or life's challenges outwardly, I thank You for Your promise of inner renewal. Revitalize my spirit, Lord.

As You renew me inwardly, let this renewal overflow into every aspect of my life. Help me to not lose heart in the face of difficulties, but to focus on the eternal reality of Your ongoing work in me. In Jesus' name, Amen.

In what ways have you experienced inward renewal recently,
and how can you cultivate more of it in your life?

Day 141: TEACH GOD'S WORD DILIGENTLY

*"These commandments that I give you today are to be
on your hearts. Impress them on your children"*
(Deuteronomy 6:6–7, NIV)

Heavenly Father, I come before You with a heart full of gratitude for Your Word. Thank You for entrusting me with the precious responsibility of teaching Your truths to my children. Help me to first internalize Your commandments, allowing them to take root deep in my own heart.

Lord, give me patience and perseverance in this vital task. Remind me of the eternal impact of sharing Your Word. Grant me wisdom and creativity in finding ways to impress Your Word upon my children's hearts in our daily lives. In Jesus' name, Amen.

**What creative ways can you incorporate God's Word
into your daily interactions with your children?**

Day 142: MODEL A LIFE OF FAITH

"But as for me and my household, we will serve the Lord."
(Joshua 24:15, NIV)

Lord God, I stand before You today, recommitting my household to Your service. Help me to lead by example, demonstrating what it means to live a life of faith. Give me the courage to make choices that honor You, even when they go against the cultural tide. May my children see in me a genuine love for You and a desire to follow Your ways.

Father, when I falter or fail, use those moments to show my children the reality of Your grace and forgiveness. Help me to be transparent about my own faith journey, sharing both victories and struggles. In Your name, I pray, Amen.

**How can you more intentionally model your faith
for your children in your daily life?**

"I have no greater joy than to hear that my children are walking in the truth"
(3 John 1:4, NIV)

Gracious Father, I lift my children up to You in prayer. You know them intimately, having formed them in the womb. I ask that You would nurture the seeds of faith in their hearts, helping them to grow strong in their relationship with You. Protect them from the doubts and temptations that may threaten their faith.

Lord, let Your Spirit intercede with groans too deep for words. Give me the patience to wait on Your timing, trusting that You are always at work in their lives. May I never cease to pray for them, rejoicing in every step they take in Your truth. In Christ's name, Amen.

**What specific aspect of your children's faith journey
can you commit to praying for regularly?**

Day 144: ENCOURAGE SPIRITUAL GROWTH

*"Like newborn babies, crave pure spiritual milk,
so that by it you may grow up in your salvation"*
(1 Peter 2:2, NIV)

Loving God, I thank You for the gift of salvation and the opportunity for continual spiritual growth. Help me to nurture in my children a hunger for Your Word and a desire to grow in their faith. Give me discernment to recognize and encourage their spiritual curiosity and growth.

Father, show me how to create an environment in our home that fosters spiritual development. Help me to be patient with their questions and doubts, seeing them as opportunities for growth rather than threats to faith. May I always point them to You as the source of true wisdom and understanding. In Jesus' name, I pray, Amen.

**How can you create more opportunities for spiritual
growth in your family's daily routine?**

"Trust in the Lord with all your heart and lean not on your own understanding"
(Proverbs 3:5, NIV)

Faithful God, I come before You, acknowledging my own need to grow in trusting You. Help me to model for my children what it means to trust You with all my heart. Give me the words and actions to teach them that Your ways are higher than our ways, and Your thoughts higher than our thoughts.

Lord, when life brings challenges or disappointments, use those moments to deepen our trust in You. Help me guide my children to see Your hand at work in all circumstances. May they learn to lean on Your understanding rather than their own, finding security and peace in Your unfailing love. In Your trustworthy name, I pray, Amen.

**What personal experience of trusting God can you
share with your children to encourage their faith?**

Day 146: NURTURE A HEART OF WORSHIP

"Worship the Lord with gladness; come before him with joyful songs"
(Psalm 100:2, NIV)

Glorious God, I praise You for Your worthiness to be worshipped. Help me to cultivate in my children's hearts that naturally turn to You in worship. May they see in me a joyful devotion to You that goes beyond mere ritual or obligation.

Father, guide me in creating moments of family worship that engage our hearts and minds. Help us to see Your glory in creation, in Your Word, and in our daily lives, responding with gladness and joyful songs. When worship feels difficult, remind us of Your constant goodness and faithfulness. In Jesus' name, Amen.

**How can you incorporate more spontaneous
moments of worship into your family life?**

"Train up a child in the way he should go; even when he is old he will not depart from it"
(Proverbs 22:6, ESV)

Wise Father, I thank You for the privilege and responsibility of training my children in Your ways. Grant me discernment to understand each child's unique bent, and wisdom to guide them along the path You have for them. Help me to instill in them values that reflect Your character and kingdom.

Lord, in a world that often promotes values contrary to Your Word, give me the courage to stand firm in teaching Your truth. Help me to explain and demonstrate godly values in ways my children can understand and embrace. Amen.

What specific godly value do you feel led to focus on instilling in your children at this time?

Week 22. Overcoming Fear and Anxiety

Day 148: TRUST IN GOD'S PROTECTION

"When I am afraid, I put my trust in you"
(Psalm 56:3, NIV)

Almighty God, in a world full of uncertainties and dangers, I turn to You as my ultimate protector. When fear creeps into my heart, help me to immediately redirect my focus to Your unfailing love and power. Remind me of the many times You've shielded me from harm and guided me through difficult situations.

Lord, strengthen my trust in You, especially in moments when I feel vulnerable or afraid. Help me to see challenges not as threats, but as opportunities to experience Your protection and grow in faith. Amen.

How can you practically demonstrate trust in God's protection when faced with a fearful situation today?

"Cast all your anxiety on him because he cares for you."
(1 Peter 5:7, NIV)

Loving Father, I come before You, carrying the weight of my worries and anxieties. Thank You for inviting me to cast all these burdens onto You. Help me to release my grip on these concerns, trusting in Your care and provision. Remind me that You are not distant or indifferent, but deeply invested in every aspect of my life.

Lord, when I'm tempted to take back my worries or doubt Your care, gently correct me. Teach me to leave my anxieties in Your capable hands, knowing that You work all things for my good. May the peace that comes from fully relying on You be evident in my life. In Christ's name, Amen.

What specific anxiety do you need to intentionally cast upon God today?

Day 150: FIND PEACE IN PRAYER

*"Do not be anxious about anything, but in every situation, by prayer
and petition, with thanksgiving, present your requests to God."*
(Philippians 4:6, NIV)

Heavenly Father, I thank You for the gift of prayer and the peace it brings. In every situation that causes me anxiety, help me to turn to You first. Guide me in presenting my requests to You with a heart full of gratitude, knowing that You hear and care about every detail of my life.

Lord, when anxious thoughts threaten to overwhelm me, remind me to pray. Help me to cultivate a habit of bringing everything to You in prayer, both big and small concerns. May the practice of prayer transform my worries into worship, my fear into faith, and my anxiety into peace that surpasses all understanding. In Jesus' name, Amen.

**How can you incorporate more thankfulness into your prayers,
especially when dealing with anxious situations?**

"For God has not given us a spirit of fear, but of power and of love and of a sound mind"
(2 Timothy 1:7, NKJV)

Mighty God, I praise You for the spirit of power, love, and sound mind that You've given me. When fear threatens to paralyze me, remind me of the resources You've placed within me. Help me to tap into Your power, to act in love, and to think with clarity and wisdom.

Lord, embolden me to step out in faith, even when fear whispers doubts. Use the challenges I face as opportunities to demonstrate Your power working through me. May my life be characterized not by timidity, but by courageous faith that inspires others to trust in You. In the name of Jesus, who conquered all fear, I pray, Amen.

**In what area of your life do you need to replace fear
with faith, power, love, or sound thinking?**

Day 152: REST IN GOD'S PRESENCE

"The Lord is with me; I will not be afraid. What can mere mortals do to me?"
(Psalm 118:6, NIV)

Omnipresent God, I thank You for Your constant presence in my life. Help me to find deep rest and security in the knowledge that You are always with me. When circumstances or people threaten to intimidate me, remind me that Your presence far outweighs any earthly power.

Lord, increase my awareness of Your presence throughout each day. In moments of fear or uncertainty, help me to pause and acknowledge that You are right here with me. May the peace that comes from resting in Your presence be evident to those around me, drawing them to seek You as their ultimate source of security. In Your powerful name, I pray, Amen.

How can you cultivate a greater awareness of God's presence in your daily life?

"So do not fear, for I am with you; do not be dismayed, for I am your God. I will strengthen you and help you; I will uphold you with my righteous right hand"
(Isaiah 41:10, NIV)

Faithful God, I thank You for the strength and comfort found in Your Word. When fear and dismay threaten to overwhelm me, help me to cling to Your promises. Remind me that You are not only with me but are actively strengthening, helping, and upholding me through every challenge.

Lord, embed Your Word deep in my heart, that I might recall Your promises in moments of fear. Help me to see beyond my circumstances to the reality of Your unfailing support. May Your Word be a constant source of courage and hope. Amen.

**Which of God's promises do you need to meditate on
and apply to a current fearful situation in your life?**

Day 154: EMBRACE GOD'S PERFECT LOVE

"There is no fear in love. But perfect love drives out fear, because fear has to do with punishment. The one who fears is not made perfect in love"
(1 John 4:18, NIV)

Loving Father, I praise You for Your perfect love that has the power to drive out all fear. Help me to fully embrace and experience the depth of Your love for me. When fear creeps in, remind me that Your love is not conditional or fleeting, but perfect and eternal.

Lord, heal any areas in my heart where fear of punishment or rejection lingers. Help me to rest securely in Your love, knowing that in Christ, I stand fully accepted and forgiven. May Your perfect love cast out fear in my life, freeing me to love You and others more fully. Let my life be a testament to the transforming power of Your love. In Jesus' name, Amen.

**How can you more fully embrace and reflect
God's perfect love in your life today?**

Day 155: CULTIVATE A SERVANT'S HEART

*"For even the Son of Man did not come to be served,
but to serve, and to give his life as a ransom for many"*
(Mark 10:45, NIV)

Lord Jesus, I am humbled by Your example of selfless service. You, the King of Kings, came not to be served but to serve. Help me to follow in Your footsteps, cultivating a heart that seeks to serve others without expecting anything in return.

Father, when my own desires and comfort threaten to overshadow the needs of others, remind me of Christ's sacrifice. Give me eyes to see opportunities to serve and the courage to step out in love. May my life be characterized by selfless service that points others to Your great love. In Jesus' name, Amen.

**How can you intentionally cultivate a servant's
heart in your daily interactions today?**

Day 156: SHOW KINDNESS TO OTHERS

*"Be kind and compassionate to one another, forgiving
each other, just as in Christ God forgave you"*
(Ephesians 4:32, NIV)

Merciful God, thank You for the kindness and compassion You've shown me through Christ. Help me to extend that same kindness to others, even when it's challenging. Give me a heart of compassion that sees beyond outward appearances to the needs and hurts of those around me.

Lord, when I'm tempted to respond with harshness or indifference, remind me of the forgiveness I've received from You. Help me to forgive freely, just as I've been forgiven. In Jesus' name, Amen.

**What specific act of kindness can you show to someone today,
especially someone who may be difficult to love?**

"Whoever is kind to the poor lends to the Lord,
and he will reward them for what they have done"
(Proverbs 19:17, NIV)

Compassionate Father, open my eyes to see the needs of those around me, especially the poor and marginalized. Give me a heart that responds with generosity and kindness. Help me to remember that when I serve those in need, I am serving You.

Lord, guard me against indifference or judgment towards those less fortunate. Instead, fill me with Your compassion and wisdom to help in ways that truly make a difference. May my actions be motivated by love, not by a desire for reward. Use me as an instrument of Your provision and care for those in need. In Jesus' name, Amen.

How can you practically care for someone in need in your community this week?

Day 158: USE YOUR GIFTS TO SERVE

"Each of you should use whatever gift you have received to serve others,
as faithful stewards of God's grace in its various forms."
(1 Peter 4:10, NIV)

Gracious God, thank You for the unique gifts and talents You've given me. Help me to recognize these gifts as tools for serving others and bringing glory to Your name. Give me wisdom to know how to use my abilities effectively in service to others.

Lord, when I'm tempted to use my gifts for selfish gain or recognition, remind me that I am a steward of Your grace. Help me to serve faithfully and joyfully, knowing that You are the source of all I have. May the use of my gifts bring encouragement to others and draw them closer to You. In Jesus' name, Amen.

What gift or talent has God given you that
you can use to serve others this week?

"Offer hospitality to one another without grumbling."
(1 Peter 4:9, NIV)

Welcoming God, thank You for the warmth and acceptance You've shown me. Help me to extend that same hospitality to others, creating spaces of welcome and belonging. Give me a heart that delights in opening my home and my life to others.

Lord, when hospitality feels inconvenient or burdensome, remind me of the joy it brings to You and others. Help me to serve with cheerfulness, seeing each guest as an opportunity to show Your love. May my hospitality be a reflection of Your open arms, inviting others into Your family. In Jesus' name, Amen.

How can you show hospitality to someone in
need of welcome or belonging this week?

Day 160: COMFORT OTHERS

"Praise be to the God and Father of our Lord Jesus Christ, the Father of compassion and the God of all comfort, who comforts us in all our troubles, so that we can comfort those in any trouble with the comfort we ourselves receive from God"
(2 Corinthians 1:3-4, NIV)

Comforting Father, I praise You for the solace and strength You provide in times of trouble. Help me to be a channel of Your comfort to those around me who are hurting. Give me sensitivity to recognize pain in others and wisdom to know how to respond.

Lord, use my own experiences of receiving Your comfort to equip me in comforting others. When I feel inadequate to help, remind me that it's Your comfort flowing through me. Amen.

Who in your life is in need of comfort,
and how can you extend God's comfort to them today?

*"Do nothing out of selfish ambition or vain conceit.
Rather, in humility value others above yourselves"*
(Philippians 2:3, NIV)

Humble Savior, I am in awe of Your example of servanthood. Help me to follow in Your footsteps, setting aside my own desires and ambitions to serve others with genuine humility. Give me the strength to value others above myself, seeing them through Your eyes of love.

Lord, when pride or the desire for recognition creeps in, remind me of Your humble sacrifice. Help me to serve quietly and faithfully, seeking only to please You rather than to gain approval from others. May my humble service be a reflection of Your character, drawing others to Your selfless love. In Jesus' name, Amen.

**In what area of your life do you need to cultivate
more humility in your service to others?**

Week 24. Pursuing Holiness in Daily Life

Day 162: SEEK GOD'S HOLINESS

"But just as he who called you is holy, so be holy in all you do."
(1 Peter 1:15, NIV)

Holy God, I stand in awe of Your perfect holiness. Thank You for calling me to reflect Your character in my daily life. Help me to understand that holiness is not just about avoiding sin, but about being set apart for Your purposes.

Lord, when the world's standards tempt me to compromise, remind me of Your high calling. Give me the courage to make choices that honor You, even when it's difficult or unpopular. May my pursuit of holiness draw others to the beauty of Your character and the transforming power of Your grace. In Jesus' name, Amen.

In what area of your life do you need to more actively pursue holiness today?

"Do not conform to the pattern of this world,
but be transformed by the renewing of your mind"
(Romans 12:2, NIV)

Transforming God, I thank You for the power to change through the renewing of my mind. Help me to recognize and resist the patterns of thinking that conform to the world's values. Fill my mind with Your truth, reshaping my thoughts to align with Your will.

Father, when worldly influences threaten to mold my thinking, draw me back to Your Word. Guide me in cultivating habits that nourish my mind with Your wisdom and perspective. May the transformation of my mind lead to a life that clearly demonstrates Your good, pleasing, and perfect will. In Jesus' name, Amen.

What specific steps can you take to renew your mind
and resist conformity to the world today?

Day 164: GUARD YOUR HEART

"Above all else, guard your heart, for everything you do flows from it"
(Proverbs 4:23, NIV)

Watchful Father, I thank You for the reminder of the importance of guarding my heart. Help me to be vigilant in protecting my inner life, knowing that it influences everything I do. Give me discernment to recognize and reject influences that could corrupt my heart.

Lord, when I'm tempted to let my guard down, remind me of the value You place on a pure heart. Help me to fill my heart with things that are true, noble, right, pure, lovely, and admirable. May the condition of my heart reflect Your love and holiness, influencing my actions and attitudes in a way that honors You. In Jesus' name, Amen.

What specific steps can you take to better guard your heart against negative in-
fluences today?

"So I say, walk by the Spirit, and you will not gratify the desires of the flesh"
(Galatians 5:16, NIV)

Holy Spirit, I thank You for Your presence in my life. Guide me in walking closely with You each moment of this day. Help me to be sensitive to Your leading, quick to obey Your promptings, and resistant to the desires of my flesh.

Lord, when I'm tempted to rely on my own strength or wisdom, remind me to depend on Your power. Fill me afresh with Your presence, producing in me the fruit of love, joy, peace, patience, kindness, goodness, faithfulness, gentleness, and self-control. May my walk in the Spirit be evident to those around me, drawing them to experience Your transforming power. In Jesus' name, Amen.

**How can you be more intentional about walking
in the Spirit throughout your day?**

Day 166: PURSUE RIGHTEOUSNESS

"But you, man of God, flee from all this, and pursue righteousness,
godliness, faith, love, endurance and gentleness"
(1 Timothy 6:11, NIV)

Righteous God, I thank You for calling me to pursue a life that reflects Your character. Give me the strength to flee from anything that compromises my walk with You. Ignite in me a passion to chase after righteousness, godliness, faith, love, endurance, and gentleness with all my heart.

Lord, when distractions or temptations try to derail my pursuit, keep my focus on You. Help me to see the pursuit of these virtues not as a burden, but as a joyful response to Your love. Amen.

**Which of these virtues do you feel particularly
called to pursue more intentionally today?**

Day 167: PRACTICE SELF-CONTROL

*"For the grace of God has appeared that offers salvation to all people.
It teaches us to say 'No' to ungodliness and worldly passions, and to
live self-controlled, upright and godly lives in this present age."*
(Titus 2:11–12, NIV)

Gracious God, I thank You for Your saving grace that not only redeems me but also teaches me to live a godly life. Help me to exercise self-control in all areas of my life, saying 'no' to ungodliness and worldly passions. Strengthen me to make choices that honor You, even when it's difficult.

Lord, when temptation feels overwhelming, remind me of the power of Your grace at work in me. Help me to see self-control not as a restriction, but as a pathway to true freedom in You. Amen.

In what area of your life do you most need to practice self-control today?

Day 168: STRIVE FOR PURITY

"Blessed are the pure in heart, for they will see God."
(Matthew 5:8, NIV)

Pure and Holy God, I thank You for the promise that the pure in heart will see You. Cleanse my heart from all impurity, and help me to strive for purity in my thoughts, motives, and actions. Give me a deeper understanding of Your holiness and a greater desire for purity in my own life.

Lord, when the world tries to compromise my purity, strengthen my resolve to remain faithful to You. Help me to guard my mind, be careful about what I allow into my heart, and make choices that reflect a commitment to purity. Amen.

What steps can you take today to cultivate greater purity in your heart and life?

Day 169: WORK AS UNTO THE LORD

*"Whatever you do, work at it with all your heart,
as working for the Lord, not for human masters"
(Colossians 3:23, NIV)*

Lord of all creation, I thank You for the gift of work and the ability to serve You through my daily tasks. Help me to approach my work with a heart fully devoted to You, recognizing that in every task, big or small, I have the opportunity to honor You.

Father, when work becomes tedious or frustrating, remind me that I'm ultimately working for You. Give me strength to persevere, integrity to do my best, and a joyful spirit that reflects Your love. In Jesus' name, Amen.

**How can you more intentionally work as unto the
Lord in your specific job or daily tasks today?**

Day 170: GOD'S GUIDANCE IN CAREER DECISIONS

*"Trust in the Lord with all your heart and lean not on your own understanding;
in all your ways submit to him, and he will make your paths straight"
(Proverbs 3:5-6, NIV)*

Wise Counselor, I come to You seeking guidance in my career path. Help me to trust in Your perfect plan for my life, even when the way forward seems unclear. Give me the courage to submit my career aspirations and decisions to You, knowing that Your ways are higher than my ways.

Lord, when I'm tempted to rely solely on my own understanding or the world's wisdom, draw me back to Your truth. Open doors that align with Your will for my life and close those that don't. May my career choices and journey be a testament to Your faithful guidance and bring glory to Your name. In Jesus' name, Amen.

What specific career decision do you need to submit to God's guidance today?

Day 171: DEMONSTRATE INTEGRITY AT WORK

"Whatever happens, conduct yourselves in a manner worthy of the gospel of Christ"
(Philippians 1:27, NIV)

Righteous God, I thank You for the opportunity to represent You in my workplace. Help me to conduct myself with integrity in all my interactions and decisions, reflecting the values of Your kingdom. Give me the strength to stand firm in my convictions, even when it's challenging.

Lord, when I face ethical dilemmas or the temptation to compromise, remind me of the gospel's worth. Help me to choose honesty over deception, kindness over harshness, and excellence over mediocrity. May my conduct at work be a clear demonstration of the transforming power of the gospel, drawing others to You. In Jesus' name, Amen.

In what specific way can you demonstrate integrity in your workplace today?

Day 172: WISDOM IN WORKPLACE CHALLENGES

"If any of you lacks wisdom, you should ask God, who gives generously
to all without finding fault, and it will be given to you"
(James 1:5, NIV)

Heavenly Father, I come before You, seeking Your divine wisdom for the challenges I face in my workplace. Thank You for the promise that You give wisdom generously when we ask. I acknowledge my need for Your guidance in navigating the complexities of my professional life.

Lord, when I encounter difficult decisions or conflicts at work, remind me to turn to You first. Give me the humility to recognize when I lack wisdom and the faith to ask You for it. Help me to trust that You will provide the insight I need, without finding fault in my shortcomings. Help me to be a light in my workplace. May I reflect your wisdom through my words and actions.

What specific workplace challenge do you need to seek God's wisdom for today?

*"In the same way, let your light shine before others, that they
may see your good deeds and glorify your Father in heaven"*
(Matthew 5:16, NIV)

Radiant Father, thank You for calling me to be a light in my workplace. Help me to shine brightly with Your love, joy, and peace in a way that draws others to You. Give me courage to stand up for You, even when it means going against the cultural tide.

Lord, when the temptation to blend in or remain silent arises, remind me of the impact my light can have. Guide me in doing good deeds that reflect Your character and point others to You. May my words, actions, and attitudes in the workplace bring glory to Your name and inspire others to seek You. In Jesus' name, Amen.

How can you intentionally shine God's light in your workplace today?

Day 174: FIND PURPOSE IN YOUR WORK

*"For we are God's handiwork, created in Christ Jesus to do good works,
which God prepared in advance for us to do"*
(Ephesians 2:10, NIV)

Creator God, I thank You for crafting me with purpose and preparing good works for me to do. Help me to see my work not just as a job, but as a calling—an opportunity to fulfill the purpose for which You created me. Give me eyes to recognize the good works You've prepared for me in my workplace.

Lord, when my work feels mundane or meaningless, remind me of the eternal significance of serving You in all I do. Help me to approach each task, interaction, and challenge as an opportunity to fulfill Your purposes. May I find deep satisfaction in knowing that my work, when done for You, has lasting value. In Jesus' name, Amen.

**How can you more fully embrace God's purpose
for you in your current work situation?**

"May the favor of the Lord our God rest on us; establish the work
of our hands for us— yes, establish the work of our hands"
(Psalm 90:17, NIV)

Gracious God, I humbly ask for Your favor to rest upon me in my workplace. Establish the work of my hands, making my efforts fruitful and impactful. Grant me success not for my own glory, but for the advancement of Your kingdom and the benefit of others.

Lord, help me to define success according to Your standards, not the world's. When I experience favor or success, keep me humble and grateful, always acknowledging You as the source of every blessing. May the favor and success You grant me open doors to share Your love and bring glory to Your name. In Jesus' name, Amen.

How can you use the favor and success God
gives you to bless others and glorify Him?

Week 26. Balancing Priorities

Day 176: PUT GOD FIRST

"But seek first his kingdom and his righteousness,
and all these things will be given to you as well"
(Matthew 6:33, NIV)

Heavenly Father, in a world full of competing demands, help me to prioritize Your kingdom and righteousness above all else. Remind me that when I put You first, everything else falls into proper perspective. Give me the wisdom to align my daily choices with Your will and purposes.

Lord, when the cares of this world threaten to overshadow my focus on You, gently redirect my attention. Help me to trust that as I seek You first, You will provide for all my needs. May my life be a testament to the peace and fulfillment that come from putting You at the center of everything. In Jesus' name, Amen.

What practical step can you take today to put God first in your life?

*"Be very careful, then, how you live—not as unwise but as wise,
making the most of every opportunity, because the days are evil."*
(Ephesians 5:15-16, NIV)

Eternal God, I thank You for the gift of time. Help me to steward this precious resource wisely, recognizing that each moment is an opportunity to honor You and make a positive impact. Grant me discernment to prioritize what truly matters in light of eternity.

Lord, when I'm tempted to waste time or become overwhelmed by busyness, guide me back to Your purposes. Help me to be intentional with my schedule, balancing work, rest, relationships, and spiritual growth. Amen.

**How can you better manage your time today
to reflect godly wisdom and priorities?**

Day 178: SET GODLY PRIORITIES

"For where your treasure is, there your heart will be also."
(Matthew 6:21, NIV)

Loving Father, help me to examine my heart and align my priorities with Your will. Show me where I've placed my treasure in things that don't truly matter, and guide me in investing in what has eternal value. Give me the courage to make changes where necessary to reflect Your priorities in my life.

Lord, when worldly pressures tempt me to misplace my priorities, remind me of what truly matters to You. Help me to treasure relationships, character growth, and kingdom work above material pursuits or worldly success. May my priorities be a clear reflection of my love for You and commitment to Your ways. In Jesus' name, Amen.

**What area of your life might need reprioritizing
to better align with God's values?**

"Come to me, all you who are weary and burdened, and I will give you rest"
(Matthew 11:28, NIV)

Peaceful Savior, I come to You weary and burdened, accepting Your invitation to find rest in Your presence. Help me to prioritize time with You, recognizing that true rest and renewal come from being in Your presence. Teach me to lay my burdens at Your feet and receive Your peace.

Lord, when life feels overwhelming, and rest seems impossible, draw me back to Your promise of rest. Help me to create margins in my life for stillness and reflection with You. May the rest I find in Your presence rejuvenate my soul and equip me to better handle life's demands. In Jesus' name, Amen.

How can you intentionally create space in your day to rest in God's presence?

"Very early in the morning, while it was still dark, Jesus got up,
left the house and went off to a solitary place, where he prayed"
(Mark 1:35, NIV)

Disciplined Savior, I am inspired by Your example of prioritizing time with the Father. Help me to cultivate consistent spiritual disciplines in my life, especially in prayer and study of Your Word. Give me the determination to prioritize these practices, even when life gets busy.

Lord, when distractions or tiredness tempt me to neglect spiritual disciplines, remind me of their importance for my spiritual growth. Help me to find creative ways to incorporate prayer, Bible study, and worship into my daily routine. May these practices deepen my relationship with You and equip me to face life's challenges. In Jesus' name, Amen.

What spiritual discipline do you feel led to
prioritize or strengthen in your life right now?

Day 181: NURTURE IMPORTANT RELATIONSHIPS

"A friend loves at all times, and a brother is born for a time of adversity"
(Proverbs 17:17, NIV)

Relational God, thank You for the gift of relationships. Help me to prioritize and nurture the important connections in my life, recognizing them as blessings from You. Give me wisdom to invest time and energy into building strong, godly relationships with family and friends.

Lord, when the busyness of life threatens to overshadow my relationships, remind me of their value. Help me to be present, supportive, and loving in my interactions with others. May the relationships I nurture be a reflection of Your love and a source of mutual encouragement and growth. In Jesus' name, Amen.

**Which relationship in your life needs more intentional
nurturing, and how can you invest in it today?**

Day 182: TRUST GOD WITH YOUR SCHEDULE

"Commit to the Lord whatever you do, and he will establish your plans"
(Proverbs 16:3, NIV)

Sovereign God, I commit my plans and schedule to You. Help me to trust You with every aspect of my day, believing that You will establish my steps according to Your perfect will. Give me the faith to hold my plans loosely, always ready to adjust to Your guidance.

Lord, when unexpected changes or disruptions occur, remind me that You are in control. Help me to approach my schedule with both diligence and flexibility, always seeking Your will above my own. May my trust in Your sovereignty over my time be evident in my peace and adaptability. In Jesus' name, Amen.

**How can you more fully commit your plans to God
and trust His guidance for your schedule today?**

Day 183: DEVELOP PATIENCE IN TRIALS

"Be patient, then, brothers and sisters, until the Lord's coming. See how the farmer waits for the land to yield its valuable crop, patiently waiting for the autumn and spring rains"
(James 5:7, NIV)

Patient Father, in a world of instant gratification, teach me the value of waiting. Help me to develop patience in the face of trials, trusting in Your perfect timing and purposes. Like a farmer waiting for crops to grow, give me the endurance to persist through difficult seasons.

Lord, when I'm tempted to rush or become discouraged in waiting, remind me of the growth that occurs during these times. Help me to see trials as opportunities for developing patience and deepening my faith in You. In Jesus' name, Amen.

How can you practice patience in a current trial or waiting period in your life?

Day 184: GENTLENESS IN RELATIONSHIPS

"Let your gentleness be evident to all. The Lord is near."
(Philippians 4:5, NIV)

Gentle Savior, help me to reflect Your gentleness in all my relationships. Soften my words, actions, and reactions, especially in challenging interactions. Remind me that gentleness is not a weakness but a powerful expression of Your character.

Lord, when I'm tempted to respond harshly or defensively, bring to mind Your nearness and the gentleness You've shown me. Help me to be a calming presence in tense situations and a source of comfort to those who are hurting. May my gentleness draw others to the beauty of Your love. In Jesus' name, Amen.

**In which relationship or situation do you need
to practice more gentleness today?**

"A gentle answer turns away wrath, but a harsh word stirs up anger"
(Proverbs 15:1, NIV)

Gracious God, grant me the strength to respond with gentleness, even when under pressure. Help me to choose my words carefully, knowing that they have the power to diffuse conflict or escalate it. Fill me with Your grace, that I might extend it to others, especially in tense moments.

Lord, when I feel provoked or frustrated, remind me of the impact of my response. Give me the self-control to pause before reacting and the wisdom to choose words that bring peace. May my gentle responses be a reflection of Your love and a tool for reconciliation in my relationships. In Jesus' name, Amen.

**How can you prepare yourself to respond with
grace in potentially tense situations today?**

Day 186: WAIT ON GOD'S TIMING

"Wait for the Lord; be strong and take heart and wait for the Lord."
(Psalm 27:14, NIV)

Eternal God, I am human with a very short-sighted perspective. I need You to teach me to wait on Your perfect timing, even when I don't see where You're leading me at the moment. Strengthen my heart as I wait, filling me with hope and trust in Your faithfulness. Help me to see waiting not as a delay, but as an active posture of faith and expectation.

Lord, when waiting feels unbearable, remind me of Your promises and Your track record of faithfulness. Use this time of waiting to deepen my reliance on You and to prepare me for what's ahead. May my patient waiting be a witness to others of Your trustworthiness and perfect timing. In Jesus' name, Amen.

**What area of your life requires patience while
waiting on God's timing right now?**

*"But the fruit of the Spirit is love, joy, peace, forbearance,
kindness, goodness, faithfulness, gentleness and self-control."*
(Galatians 5:22-23, NIV)

Holy Spirit, I invite You to produce Your fruit in my life. Cultivate in me a character that reflects Your nature – full of love, joy, peace, patience, kindness, goodness, faithfulness, gentleness, and self-control. Help me to cooperate with Your work in my life, yielding to Your transforming power.

Lord, when I struggle with impatience or harshness, remind me to rely on Your strength rather than my own. Help me to see each challenge as an opportunity for Your fruit to grow in my life. May the fruit of Your Spirit in me be a sweet aroma that draws others to You. In Jesus' name, Amen.

Which fruit of the Spirit do you most need to cultivate in your life right now?

Day 188: SHOW PATIENCE IN DIFFICULT SITUATIONS

"Be completely humble and gentle; be patient, bearing with one another in love"
(Ephesians 4:2, NIV)

Patient Lord, give me the strength to bear with others in love, especially in difficult situations. Help me to approach challenges with humility and gentleness, remembering the patience You've shown me. Grant me the grace to extend understanding and forbearance to those who test my patience.

Father, when I'm tempted to react with frustration or anger, remind me of Your call to love patiently. Help me to see others through Your eyes of compassion and to respond with kindness, even when it's difficult. May my patient love be a reflection of Your character and a powerful witness to Your transforming grace. In Jesus' name, Amen.

**In what specific situation or relationship do y
ou need to practice more patience today?**

*"Being confident of this, that he who began a good work in you
will carry it on to completion until the day of Christ Jesus"*
(Philippians 1:6, NIV)

Faithful God, I thank You for the good work You've begun in me. Help me to trust in Your ongoing process of transformation, even when progress seems slow or difficult. Give me patience with myself and with Your timing as You continue to shape me into the image of Christ.

Lord, when I grow impatient with my own growth or the growth of others, remind me of Your promise to complete what You've started. Help me to cooperate with Your work in my life, submitting to Your refining process. May my confidence in Your faithfulness encourage others to trust in Your transforming power. In Jesus' name, Amen.

**How can you more fully trust and cooperate with
God's process of growth in your life today?**

July

Week 28. Embracing God's Grace in Imperfection

Day 190: GOD'S UNCONDITIONAL LOVE

*"But God demonstrates his own love for us in this:
While we were still sinners, Christ died for us"*
(Romans 5:8, NIV)

Loving Father, I am overwhelmed by the depth of Your love for me. Help me to fully embrace and accept Your unconditional love, especially when I feel unworthy or unlovable. Remind me that Your love is not based on my performance or perfection, but on Your unchanging character.

Lord, when I struggle with self-doubt or guilt, draw me back to the truth of Your sacrificial love demonstrated through Christ. Help me to live in the freedom and security of Your love. In Jesus' name, Amen.

How can you more fully accept and live in God's unconditional love today?

*"But he said to me, 'My grace is sufficient for you, for my power
is made perfect in weakness.' Therefore I will boast all the more gladly
about my weaknesses, so that Christ's power may rest on me"*
(2 Corinthians 12:9, NIV)

Gracious God, I thank You that Your strength is made perfect in my weakness. Help me to embrace my limitations and imperfections, recognizing them as opportunities for Your power to shine through. Give me the courage to be vulnerable about my weaknesses, trusting in Your all-sufficient grace.

Lord, when I'm tempted to hide my struggles or rely on my own strength, remind me that Your grace is enough. May my weaknesses become a testament to Your strength and a source of encouragement to others who are struggling. In Jesus' name, Amen.

In what area of weakness do you need to rely more fully on God's strength today?

Day 192: EMBRACE FORGIVENESS

*"If we confess our sins, he is faithful and just and will forgive
us our sins and purify us from all unrighteousness"*
(1 John 1:9, NIV)

Merciful Father, I come before You, acknowledging my need for forgiveness. Thank You for Your promise to forgive and purify me when I confess my sins. Help me to embrace Your forgiveness fully, letting go of guilt and shame, and walking in the freedom You provide.

Lord, when I struggle to forgive myself or accept Your forgiveness, remind me of the completeness of Your grace. Give me the courage to confess my sins honestly and the faith to receive Your forgiveness wholeheartedly. In Jesus' name, Amen.

**Is there an area in your life where you need to
more fully embrace God's forgiveness?**

*"Consider it pure joy, my brothers and sisters, whenever you face trials of many kinds,
because you know that the testing of your faith produces perseverance"*
(James 1:2-3, NIV)

Sovereign God, I thank You for the growth that comes through challenges. Help me to embrace difficulties not as punishments, but as opportunities for spiritual growth and character development. Give me the perspective to see Your hand at work even in my struggles.

Lord, when I face trials, remind me of Your promise to use them for my good. Grant me the strength to persevere and the wisdom to learn the lessons You have for me in each challenge. May my response to difficulties be a testimony to Your faithfulness and a source of encouragement to others facing their own trials. In Jesus' name, Amen.

**How can you approach a current challenge
in your life as an opportunity for growth?**

Day 194: RELY ON GOD'S STRENGTH

"I can do all this through him who gives me strength."
(Philippians 4:13, NIV)

Almighty God, I acknowledge my dependence on Your strength. Help me to rely not on my own abilities, but on Your power working through me. In moments of weakness or self-doubt, remind me that with You, all things are possible.

Lord, when tasks seem overwhelming or goals unattainable, help me to lean into Your strength. Give me the faith to step out boldly, trusting not in my own capabilities but in Your unlimited power. May my reliance on Your strength be evident in my actions and attitudes, inspiring others to trust in You. In Jesus' name, Amen.

**In what specific area of your life do you need
to rely more fully on God's strength today?**

*"Let us then approach God's throne of grace with confidence, so that we
may receive mercy and find grace to help us in our time of need"*
(Hebrews 4:16, NIV)

Merciful Father, I thank You for inviting me to approach Your throne with confidence. Help me to fully accept and embrace Your mercy, especially in times when I feel undeserving. Give me the courage to come to You with all my needs, trusting in Your compassion and grace.

Lord, when shame or fear hold me back from seeking Your help, remind me of Your open arms of mercy. Help me to live in the freedom that comes from knowing I can always turn to You for grace and assistance. May my confidence in Your mercy inspire others to seek Your help in their time of need. In Jesus' name, Amen.

**How can you more confidently approach God's
throne of grace with a current need in your life?**

Day 196: TRUST IN GOD'S PLAN

*"And we know that in all things God works for the good of those
who love him, who have been called according to his purpose"*
(Romans 8:28, NIV)

Sovereign Lord, I thank You for Your promise to work all things for my good. Help me to trust in Your perfect plan, even when circumstances seem challenging or confusing. Give me faith to believe that You are always working behind the scenes, weaving even my mistakes and imperfections into Your beautiful tapestry.

Father, when doubt or disappointment threatens my trust in Your plan, remind me of Your faithfulness throughout history and in my own life. Help me to surrender my own agenda and embrace Your purposes, knowing that Your ways are higher than my ways. In Jesus' name, Amen.

In what area of your life do you need to more fully trust God's plan today?

Day 197: APPRECIATE FATHERLY WISDOM

"Listen, my son, to your father's instruction and do not forsake your mother's teaching"
(Proverbs 1:8, NIV)

Heavenly Father, I thank You for the gift of fatherly wisdom. Help me to appreciate and value the instruction and guidance that fathers provide. Open my heart to receive their wisdom with humility and gratitude.

Lord, when I'm tempted to disregard fatherly advice, remind me of the importance of honoring this wisdom. Give me discernment to recognize the valuable life lessons passed down through generations. May I not only listen but also apply this wisdom in my daily life, becoming a channel of godly wisdom for future generations. In Jesus' name, Amen.

What specific wisdom have you received from your father or father figure?

Day 198: HONOR FATHERS WITH RESPECT

"Honor your father and your mother, so that you may
live long in the land the Lord your God is giving you"
(Exodus 20:12, NIV)

Gracious God, thank You for the commandment to honor our fathers. Help me to show genuine respect and appreciation for my father or father figure, recognizing the role they play in my life. Give me the strength to honor them even in challenging times.

Lord, when relationships are strained or imperfect, guide me in finding ways to show respect and honor. Help me to focus on the positive aspects of our relationship and to extend grace where needed. May my actions and attitudes towards my father be a reflection of Your love and a fulfillment of Your commandment. In Jesus' name, Amen.

In what specific way can you show honor and
respect to your father or father figure today?

"As a father has compassion on his children,
so the Lord has compassion on those who fear him"
(Psalm 103:13, NIV)

Loving Father, I praise You for being the perfect example of fatherhood. Help me to see and appreciate Your fatherly compassion in my life. Deepen my understanding of Your unconditional love and endless patience towards me.

Lord, when earthly fathers fall short, remind me of Your perfect fatherhood. Help me to find comfort and security in Your unfailing love. May my relationship with You as my Heavenly Father bring healing to any Father wound I may carry and enable me to extend grace to imperfect earthly fathers. In Jesus' name, Amen.

How can you more fully embrace God's perfect fatherhood in your life today?

Day 200: PRAY FOR SPIRITUAL LEADERSHIP

"Fathers, do not exasperate your children; instead, bring
them up in the training and instruction of the Lord"
(Ephesians 6:4, NIV)

Almighty God, I lift up all fathers to You, asking for Your guidance in their role as spiritual leaders. I especially pray for the fathers in my family. Grant them wisdom, patience, and courage to lead their families in Your ways. Help them to balance discipline with love, and instruction with understanding.

Lord, for fathers who struggle with this responsibility, I ask for Your empowerment and grace. Guide them in creating an atmosphere of love and spiritual growth in their homes. May their leadership reflect Your character and draw their children closer to You. In Jesus' name, Amen.

How can you support or encourage a father in his role as a spiritual leader today?

Day 201: APPRECIATE FATHERLY PROTECTION

"The righteous lead blameless lives; blessed are their children after them"
(Proverbs 20:7, NIV)

Protective Father, I thank You for the security and protection that fathers provide. Help me to appreciate the sacrifices and efforts fathers make to ensure the safety and well-being of their families. Give me a heart of gratitude for this often unspoken aspect of fatherhood.

Lord, for fathers who strive to lead righteous lives, I ask for Your continued strength and guidance. Help them to understand the lasting impact of their integrity on their children. May their example of righteousness be a shield and a blessing to their families for generations to come. In Jesus' name, Amen.

**How can you express appreciation for the protection
and security provided by your father or father figure?**

Day 202: HONOR FATHERS THROUGH OBEDIENCE

"Children, obey your parents in the Lord, for this is right."
(Ephesians 6:1, NIV)

Heavenly Father, I thank You for the instruction to honor fathers through obedience. Thank you for giving me an earthly father so that I could somehow grasp Your being a Father to me. Help me to respond to fatherly guidance with a willing and obedient heart. Give me the humility to submit to authority. I understand that this honors both my earthly father and You.

Lord, I know that there are times when it's hard for me to obey. My earthly father is not perfect, but You, Lord, my perfect Father in Heaven, tells me to honor him for Your sake. Help me to trust that You work through the authority structures You've established. In Jesus' name, Amen.

**In what area of your life do you need to practice
obedience to honor your father or father figure?**

"The father of a righteous child has great joy;
a man who fathers a wise son rejoices in him"
(Proverbs 23:24, NIV)

Loving God, I thank You for the gift of fatherly love. Help me to recognize and appreciate the joy that fathers experience in their children's growth and success. Give me a deeper understanding of the emotional investment fathers make in their children's lives.

Lord, for fathers who struggle to express their love, I ask for Your help in breaking down barriers. Open channels of communication and affection in father-child relationships. May the mutual joy between fathers and children be a reflection of Your delight in us, Your children. In Jesus' name, Amen.

How can you bring joy to your father's heart
through your actions or words today?

Week 30. Praying for the Global Church and Missions

Day 204: EMBRACE THE GREAT COMMISSION

"Therefore go and make disciples of all nations, baptizing them in
the name of the Father and of the Son and of the Holy Spirit."
(Matthew 28:19, NIV)

Lord Jesus, I thank You for entrusting us with the Great Commission. Ignite in me a passion for sharing Your gospel with all nations. Give me courage to step out of my comfort zone and the wisdom to share Your love effectively across cultural boundaries.

Father, open my eyes to opportunities for fulfilling this commission in my daily life. Whether through going, sending, or supporting, help me play my part in making disciples of all nations. In Jesus' name, Amen.

How can you actively participate in fulfilling the Great Commission today?

*"Remember those in prison as if you were together with them in prison,
and those who are mistreated as if you yourselves were suffering"*
(Hebrews 13:3, NIV)

Heavenly Father, I lift up persecuted believers around the world. Grant them strength, courage, and hope in the face of opposition and suffering. Help them to stand firm in their faith, knowing that You are with them in their trials.

Lord, give me a heart of compassion for my persecuted brothers and sisters. Help me to remember them in prayer and to support them in practical ways. Use their faithful witness to inspire and strengthen the global church. May their perseverance bring glory to Your name and draw others to faith in You. In Jesus' name, Amen.

How can you actively support and pray for persecuted believers today?

Day 206: SUPPORT GLOBAL EVANGELISM

*"How, then, can they call on the one they have not believed in?
And how can they believe in the one of whom they have not heard?
And how can they hear without someone preaching to them?"*
(Romans 10:14, NIV)

Gracious God, I thank You for the gift of salvation through Jesus Christ. Stir in me a deep concern for those who have not yet heard the gospel. Give me a heart for global evangelism, and show me how I can support efforts to spread Your word worldwide.

Lord, raise up faithful preachers and evangelists to reach the unreached. Empower them with Your Spirit and grant them favor as they share Your truth. Open doors for the gospel in closed countries and soften hearts to receive Your message. In Jesus' name, Amen.

In what way can you support global evangelism efforts today?

"Make every effort to keep the unity of the Spirit through the bond of peace"
(Ephesians 4:3, NIV)

Prince of Peace, I pray for unity in Your global church. Break down walls of division and heal rifts that separate Your people. Help us to focus on what unites us in Christ rather than on our differences.

Lord, give church leaders wisdom and humility to work towards unity. Help all believers to embrace diversity within the body of Christ while maintaining the unity of the Spirit. May our love for one another and our unity be a powerful witness to the world of Your transforming love. In Jesus' name, Amen.

**How can you promote unity within your local church
and the broader Christian community today?**

Day 208: INTERCEDE FOR MISSIONARIES

"And pray in the Spirit on all occasions with all kinds of prayers and requests.
With this in mind, be alert and always keep on praying for all the Lord's people"
(Ephesians 6:18, NIV)

Faithful God, I lift up missionaries serving around the world. Protect them from harm, provide for their needs, and empower them with Your Spirit. Grant them wisdom in navigating cultural challenges and effectiveness in sharing Your love.

Lord, comfort missionaries in times of loneliness or discouragement. Strengthen their families and bless their ministries with fruit. Help me to be faithful in praying for and supporting missionaries. May their dedication and sacrifice inspire the church to greater commitment to Your global mission. In Jesus' name, Amen.

How can you more actively support and pray for missionaries?

*"All Scripture is God-breathed and is useful for teaching,
rebuking, correcting and training in righteousness"*
(2 Timothy 3:16, NIV)

Heavenly Father, I thank You for the gift of Your Word. I pray for ongoing efforts to translate the Bible into every language. Provide resources, technology, and skilled translators to make Your Word accessible to all people groups.

Lord, protect and guide those involved in Bible translation work, especially in challenging or dangerous areas. Help believers to treasure Your Word and to support efforts to make it available to others. May Your Word transform lives and communities as it becomes accessible in heart languages around the world. In Jesus' name, Amen.

**How can you support Bible translation efforts
or engage more deeply with Scripture?**

Day 210: SPIRITUAL AWAKENING

*"Ask me, and I will make the nations your inheritance,
the ends of the earth your possession"*
(Psalm 2:8, NIV)

Sovereign Lord, today, I just want to pray for the entire world. I ask for a global spiritual awakening. Pour out Your Spirit on all flesh, bringing conviction of sin and revelation of Your truth. Spark revival fires in every nation, drawing multitudes to faith in Jesus Christ.

Father, use global events and challenges to turn hearts towards You. Empower Your Church to boldly proclaim the gospel in this crucial time. May Your kingdom come, and Your will be done on earth as it is in heaven. Let the nations become the inheritance of Christ, and may the ends of the earth experience Your salvation. In Jesus' name, Amen.

**How can you participate in working towards spiritual
awakening in your community and beyond?**

Day 211: APPRECIATE GOD'S CREATION

"The heavens declare the glory of God; the skies proclaim the work of his hands"
(Psalm 19:1, NIV)

Creator God, open my eyes to the beauty of Your creation all around me. Help me to pause and marvel at the intricate details of nature that reflect Your glory. From the vastness of the skies to the delicacy of a flower, may I see Your handiwork in everything.

Lord, when I'm caught up in the busyness of life, remind me to take time to appreciate the world You've made. Let the beauty of creation fill me with joy and lead me to praise You. May my appreciation for Your creation inspire me to be a better steward of this amazing gift. In Jesus' name, Amen.

How can you take time today to appreciate and enjoy God's creation?

Day 212: CULTIVATE CONTENTMENT

"I have learned to be content whatever the circumstances."
(Philippians 4:11, NIV)

Gracious Father, teach me the secret of being content in all circumstances. Help me to find joy and satisfaction in what I have, rather than always longing for more. Give me the wisdom to recognize the blessings in my life, both big and small.

Lord, when discontentment creeps into my heart, remind me of Your faithfulness and provision. Help me to trust in Your goodness, knowing that You provide all I truly need. May my contentment be a powerful witness to others of Your sufficiency in my life. In Jesus' name, Amen.

In what area of your life do you need to cultivate more contentment today?

"How good and pleasant it is when God's people live together in unity!"
(Psalm 133:1, NIV)

Loving God, thank You for the gift of fellowship with others. You love us and want us to love each other as well. Please give me a heart that values unity. When opportunities for fellowship and friendship come my way, help me to welcome new people into my life. Help me to appreciate and nurture the relationships You've placed in my life.

Lord, when conflicts or differences arise, help me to prioritize unity and seek reconciliation. Help me seek to build others up in love. Teach me to find joy in the simple pleasure of spending time with others, and sharing life's ups and downs. May the fellowship I experience with other believers be a reflection of Your love and a source of encouragement to all. In Jesus' name, Amen.

How can you intentionally cultivate meaningful fellowship with others today?

Day 214: FIND JOY IN SERVING

"Serve wholeheartedly, as if you were serving the Lord, not people"
(Ephesians 6:7, NIV)

Servant King, You came to Earth to show us what it means to serve. Help me to emulate your humility and compassion. Help me find joy in serving others as an expression of my love for You. Give me a willing heart and cheerful attitude in all the tasks before me today, whether big or small. Remind me that every act of service is an opportunity to honor You.

Lord, when serving feels burdensome, renew my perspective. Help me to see the eternal significance in everyday acts of kindness and service. Let me serve joyfully and help me inspire others to discover the fulfillment that comes from giving of themselves. In Jesus' name, Amen.

What opportunity do you have today to serve others with joy?

*"Every good and perfect gift is from above, coming down from the Father
of the heavenly lights, who does not change like shifting shadows"
(James 1:17, NIV)*

Generous Father, You are the source of every good thing in my life. But sometimes, I take your gifts for granted. Please open my eyes to recognize and appreciate the many blessings You pour into my life each day. From the air I breathe to the love of family and friends, help me to see Your good gifts in everything.

Lord, when I'm tempted to take Your blessings for granted, remind me of their source. Cultivate in me a heart of gratitude that overflows with thanksgiving for both the extraordinary and the ordinary gifts in my life. May my appreciation for Your daily blessings increase my trust in Your unchanging goodness. In Jesus' name, Amen.

What often-overlooked blessings can you pause to appreciate today?

Day 216: EMBRACE LAUGHTER AND HAPPINESS

*"A cheerful heart is good medicine, but a crushed spirit dries up the bones"
(Proverbs 17:22, NIV)*

Joyful God, thank You for the gift of laughter and happiness. Help me to embrace the simple joys of life, finding reasons to smile and laugh even in challenging times. Fill my heart with Your joy that transcends circumstances.

Lord, when life feels heavy, remind me of the healing power of a cheerful heart. Help me to cultivate relationships and activities that bring genuine happiness into my life. May my joy and laughter be a reflection of the ultimate joy You have brought into my life. In Jesus' name, Amen.

How can you intentionally bring more laughter and cheerfulness into your day?

"Better a little with the fear of the Lord than great wealth with turmoil"
(Proverbs 15:16, NIV)

Prince of Peace, what a comfort it is to know that I do not have to own many things to be satisfied in life. Help me to find contentment and joy in a simple life centered on You. Free me from the constant pursuit of more, and teach me to appreciate the peace that comes from living with less. Give me the wisdom to prioritize what truly matters in light of eternity.

Lord, when I'm tempted by materialism or complexity, draw me back to the beauty of simplicity. Help me to declutter not just my physical space, but also my schedule and my mind. Your sufficient grace is all I need to be truly satisfied with the life You gave me. In Jesus' name, Amen.

**What area of your life could benefit from more simplicity,
and how can you pursue that today?**

August

Week 32. Cultivating a Heart of Worship

Day 218: PRAISE GOD IN ALL CIRCUMSTANCES

"Rejoice always, pray continually, give thanks in all circumstances;
for this is God's will for you in Christ Jesus"
(1 Thessalonians 5:16-18, NIV)

Heavenly Father, teach me to rejoice always, pray continually, and give thanks in all circumstances. When life is challenging, help me to see beyond my struggles and find reasons to praise You. May my worship be a constant melody in my heart, regardless of my situation.

Lord, when I'm tempted to complain or despair, remind me of Your faithfulness and goodness. Help me to cultivate an attitude of gratitude and a spirit of praise that perseveres through every season. Let my consistent worship be a testimony to Your unchanging nature and a source of strength for myself and others. In Jesus' name, Amen.

How can you intentionally praise God in a challenging circumstance today?

"Love the Lord your God with all your heart and with all your
soul and with all your mind and with all your strength"
(Mark 12:30, NIV)

Loving God, I am in awe of Your unmeasurable love and holiness. Truly, I cannot worship You enough. I desire to love and worship You with all my heart, soul, mind, and strength. Help me to engage every part of my being in adoration of You. May my thoughts, emotions, decisions, and actions all align to express my love and reverence for You.

Lord, when my worship becomes half-hearted or routine, reignite my passion for You. Help me to discover new ways to express my devotion and to grow deeper in my relationship with You. May my whole-hearted worship inspire others to seek You more earnestly. In Jesus' name, Amen.

In what new way can you express your worship to
God today, engaging your whole being?

Day 220: EXPRESS GRATITUDE IN WORSHIP

"Enter his gates with thanksgiving and his courts with praise;
give thanks to him and praise his name"
(Psalm 100:4, NIV)

Gracious Father, I enter Your presence with thanksgiving and Your courts with praise. You have done so much in my life that I could not even begin to count them. Open my eyes to see the countless reasons I have to be grateful. Let gratitude be the foundation of my worship, recognizing all You have done and continue to do in my life.

Lord, when I'm prone to focus on what I lack, shift my attention to the abundance of Your blessings. Help me to cultivate a habit of expressing thankfulness in my prayers, songs, and daily life. May my grateful heart overflow in joyful worship that honors You and encourages others. In Jesus' name, Amen.

What specific blessings can you thank God for in your worship today?

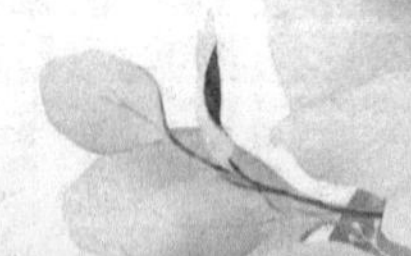

"But if serving the Lord seems undesirable to you, then choose for yourselves this day whom you will serve... But as for me and my household, we will serve the Lord"
(Joshua 24:15, NIV)

Sovereign Lord, I choose this day to serve You. You alone deserve my best. You give my life purpose and meaning. Help me to obey you with my decisions and actions. Please accept my obedience as an act of worship and as an expression of my love and reverence for You. Give me the courage to follow Your ways, even when it's difficult or unpopular.

Father, when I'm tempted to compromise or go my own way, remind me that true worship involves surrendering my will to Yours. Help me to see each act of obedience as an opportunity to honor You. May my life of faithful service be a living testimony of Your lordship and goodness. In Jesus' name, Amen.

In what area of your life is God calling you to worship through obedience today?

Day 222: EXALT GOD'S NAME

"Lord, our Lord, how majestic is your name in all the earth!"
(Psalm 8:1, NIV)

Majestic Lord, how excellent is Your name in all the earth! My heart sings praises to You, Jesus! You have created me and saved me. Your name is above every name. Help me to continually exalt Your name through my words, thoughts, and actions. May my life be a constant proclamation of Your greatness and glory.

Father, when I'm tempted to seek my own glory or the approval of others, redirect my focus to the exaltation of Your name. Help me to see opportunities throughout my day to speak of Your Majesty and to reflect Your character. In Jesus' name, Amen.

**How can you intentionally exalt God's name
in your interactions with others today?**

"Yet a time is coming and has now come when the true worshipers will worship the Father in the Spirit and in truth, for they are the kind of worshipers the Father seeks"
(John 4:23, NIV)

Holy Spirit, guide me in worshiping the Father in spirit and in truth. Help me to engage both my heart and my mind in authentic adoration. May my worship be sincere, rooted in a genuine relationship with You, and aligned with the truth of Your Word.

Lord, when my worship becomes mechanical or disconnected, revive my spirit and deepen my understanding of Your truth. Help me to cultivate a lifestyle of worship that goes beyond religious rituals to heartfelt devotion. May my sincere worship draw others into a deeper experience of Your presence. In Jesus' name, Amen.

How can you cultivate more authenticity and depth in your worship today?

Day 224: OFFER A SACRIFICE OF PRAISE

"Through Jesus, therefore, let us continually offer to God a sacrifice of praise— the fruit of lips that openly profess his name."
(Hebrews 13:15, NIV)

Jesus, through You, I offer to God a continual sacrifice of praise. Even when it's difficult, help me to declare Your goodness and profess Your name. May the fruit of my lips be a sweet offering to You, regardless of my circumstances.

Lord, when praise doesn't come easily, remind me of the power of choosing to worship despite my feelings. Help me to push through resistance and offer You praise as an act of faith and obedience. May my sacrifice of praise strengthen my faith and be a witness to Your worthiness. In Your name, I pray, Amen.

In what challenging situation can you offer a sacrifice of praise to God today?

Day 225: TRUST GOD'S TIMING

"There is a time for everything, and a season for every activity under the heavens"
(Ecclesiastes 3:1, NIV)

Eternal God, I acknowledge that there is a time for everything under heaven. Help me to trust in Your perfect timing, especially when life feels uncertain or when change is on the horizon. Give me the patience to wait for Your appointed seasons and wisdom to recognize them when they come.

Lord, when I'm tempted to rush ahead or lag behind, align my steps with Your divine schedule. Help me to embrace each season of life, knowing that You are working out Your purposes in and through me. May my trust in Your timing be a source of peace for myself and an encouragement to others. In Jesus' name, Amen.

In what area of your life do you need to trust God's timing more fully today?

Day 226: EMBRACE NEW BEGINNINGS

"See, I am doing a new thing! Now it springs up; do you not perceive it?
I am making a way in the wilderness and streams in the wasteland."
(Isaiah 43:19, NIV)

Creative God, I thank You for the new things You are doing in my life. Open my eyes to perceive the fresh starts and opportunities You're providing. Give me courage to step into new beginnings, trusting in Your guidance and provision.

Lord, when fear of the unknown tempts me to cling to the familiar, remind me of Your faithfulness in past transitions. Help me to cooperate with the new work You're doing, even when it means leaving my comfort zone. May I embrace change with faith and excitement, knowing that You are making a way for me. In Jesus' name, Amen.

What new beginning is God inviting you to embrace today?

*"The Lord himself goes before you and will be with you; he will never
leave you nor forsake you. Do not be afraid; do not be discouraged"*
(Deuteronomy 31:8, NIV)

Faithful Father, as I face transitions, I take comfort in knowing that You go before me and are with me. When change brings uncertainty or fear, remind me of Your promise to never leave or forsake me. Fill me with Your strength and courage to face new challenges.

Lord, help me to see transitions not as threats, but as opportunities for growth and deeper reliance on You. Guide my steps, calm my anxieties, and help me to trust in Your constant presence through every change. May my confidence in You during transitions be a witness to Your faithfulness. In Jesus' name, Amen.

**How can you lean on God's strength as you
navigate a current transition in your life?**

Day 228: GROW THROUGH CHALLENGES

*"Not only so, but we also glory in our sufferings,
because we know that suffering produces perseverance"*
(Romans 5:3, NIV)

Sovereign God, You have given me so many reasons to celebrate, including the challenges that I sometimes try to avoid. Help me to embrace difficulties not as obstacles, but as opportunities for developing perseverance and character. Give me the strength to endure and the wisdom to learn from every trial.

Lord, when I'm tempted to complain about hardships, remind me of the spiritual muscles being built through endurance. Help me to maintain an eternal perspective, seeing how You use challenges to shape me more into the image of Christ. May my response to difficulties inspire others to trust in Your refining process. In Jesus' name, Amen.

What challenge are you facing that you can view as an opportunity for growth?

"Forget the former things; do not dwell on the past."
(Isaiah 43:18, NIV)

Redeeming God, help me to forget the former things and not dwell on the past. Give me the strength to release hurts, regrets, and old patterns that hold me back from embracing the future You have for me. Fill me with hope and anticipation for what lies ahead.

Lord, when memories of past failures or wounds threaten to paralyze me, remind me of Your power to make all things new. Help me to learn from the past without being bound by it. May my willingness to move forward in faith inspire others to trust in Your redemptive work. In Jesus' name, Amen.

**What aspect of your past do you need to release
in order to move forward with God?**

Day 230: EMBRACE GOD'S PLAN

*"For I know the plans I have for you," declares the Lord, "plans to prosper
you and not to harm you, plans to give you hope and a future."*
(Jeremiah 29:11, NIV)

Loving Father, I thank You for Your good plans for my life. Help me to trust in Your promise of a hope-filled future, even when circumstances seem uncertain. Give me faith to embrace Your plan, knowing that You work all things for my good and Your glory.

Lord, when doubts arise or when Your plan differs from my expectations, remind me of Your loving wisdom and perfect knowledge. Help me to surrender my own agenda and to actively participate in the unfolding of Your purposes for my life. May my trust in Your plan be a testimony to Your goodness and faithfulness. In Jesus' name, Amen.

**How can you more fully embrace and cooperate
with God's plan for your life today?**

"Jesus Christ is the same yesterday and today and forever"
(Hebrews 13:8, NIV)

Unchanging God, I thank You that You remain the same yesterday, today, and forever. In the midst of life's changes, you anchor my soul in the constancy of Your character and love. Help me to always cling to Your unchanging nature as my source of peace and stability.

Lord, many times, the world around me feels chaotic or unpredictable. I get overcome by worries and fear. Draw my focus back to Your eternal truths. Help me to build my life on the solid foundation of Your unchanging Word and promises. May the peace I find in Your constancy be a beacon of hope to those navigating turbulent times. In Jesus' name, Amen.

How can you remind yourself of God's unchanging
nature in the face of change today?

Week 34. Praying for Children's Future

Day 232: ENTRUST CHILDREN TO GOD'S CARE

"Start children off on the way they should go,
and even when they are old they will not turn from it"
(Proverbs 22:6, NIV)

Heavenly Father, thank you for the life you have entrusted in my care. I desire good things to come their way. Guide me in starting them off on the right path, rooted in Your truth and love. Help me to train them up to be good Christians so that they never wander away from You when they're grown.

Lord, You know I sometimes feel inadequate or uncertain in guiding them. But I am grateful that You are here helping me. Help me to consistently model faith and point them towards You. May the seeds of faith planted in their youth grow strong and bear fruit throughout their lives. In Jesus' name, Amen.

How can you intentionally guide a child towards God's path today?

*"If any of you lacks wisdom, you should ask God, who gives generously
to all without finding fault, and it will be given to you"*
(James 1:5, NIV)

Wise God, I trust that You delight in giving us wisdom, so thank you, Lord, because You are there to guide me. I ask for Your wisdom in raising and influencing the children in my life. Pour out Your wisdom generously upon me and upon them. Help me to make decisions that align with Your will and to guide them with godly counsel.

Lord, when I lack understanding or face challenging situations with children, prompt me to seek Your wisdom first. May the wisdom You provide not only benefit the children but also draw them closer to You. In Jesus' name, Amen.

In what specific area do you need God's wisdom regarding a child in your life?

"The Lord will watch over your coming and going both now and forevermore"
(Psalm 121:8, NIV)

Protective Father, I pray for Your watchful care over the children in my life. I love my children very much, and I know You love them even more. Help me not to worry about their future because You are there for them. Guard their coming and going, their physical safety, and their spiritual well-being. Shield them from harm and negative influences that could lead them astray.

Lord, when fears for their safety arise, remind me of Your constant presence and protection. Help me to trust You with their lives while also being a responsible caregiver. As I do my best to take good care of them, I trust that You are holding them in Your gentle hands. Amen.

**What specific prayer can you commit to praying
daily for the safety and well-being of children?**

"I have no greater joy than to hear that my children are walking in the truth"
(3 John 1:4, NIV)

Faithful God, I entrust my children's spiritual growth in Your hands. I can only help introduce You to them, but only You can truly work in their hearts. Please help them develop a strong, personal faith in You that withstands life's challenges. Give them hearts that seek after You and minds that trust in Your truth.

Lord, when doubts or questions arise, use these as opportunities to deepen their faith. The world will throw so many lies at them. So, please help me to guide them towards a genuine relationship with You right now, while they are still under my care. Help them to grow in faith and inspire others to seek You. In Jesus' name, Amen.

**What steps can you take to encourage the
faith development of a child in your life?**

Day 236: GUIDANCE FOR THEIR FUTURE

*"For I know the plans I have for you," declares the Lord, "plans to prosper
you and not to harm you, plans to give you hope and a future."*
(Jeremiah 29:11, NIV)

Sovereign Lord, I lift up the future of the children in my life to You. I trust in Your good plans for them - plans to prosper them and not to harm them, plans to give them hope and a future. Guide their paths and help them to discover Your purpose for their lives.

Father, I admit that I am sometimes worried about their future. Remind me to trust in Your perfect plan. Give me the wisdom and grace to encourage their dreams while teaching them to seek Your will above all. May their lives unfold according to Your divine purpose. Amen.

How can you help a child in your life seek God's guidance for their future?

"Walk with the wise and become wise, for a companion of fools suffers harm"
(Proverbs 13:20, NIV)

Relational God, I pray for the friendships and relationships of the children in my life. Surround them with wise companions who will encourage their faith and character. Lord, shield them from those who would lead them astray, and illuminate their path with Your guidance as they form bonds that honor You.

Help me show them what healthy relationships look like and give me the wisdom to help them choose good friends. Let their relationships be full of growth, support, and happiness, bringing them closer to You. Thank You for the positive people You place in their lives. In Jesus' name, Amen.

How can you encourage positive relationships for a child in your life?

Day 238: ASK FOR GOD'S FAVOR

"May the favor of the Lord our God rest on us; establish the work
of our hands for us— yes, establish the work of our hands"
(Psalm 90:17, NIV)

Gracious Father, I pray that Your favor gently rests upon the children in my life. Help them in all their endeavors and let the work of their hands prosper with Your blessing. May Your kindness and mercy accompany them throughout their journey.

Lord, show me how to guide them in seeking Your favor above all worldly achievements. Teach them to use their talents and opportunities to honor You and bring blessings to others. Let Your favor in their lives be a shining testament to Your grace and love. Thank You for always being there for them, showering them with Your endless love. In Jesus' name, Amen.

How can you help a child in your life recognize and appreciate God's favor?

Day 239: RECOGNIZE YOUR UNIQUE GIFTS

"We have different gifts, according to the grace given to each of us"
(Romans 12:6, NIV)

Creative God, thank You for the unique gifts You've given me. Help me to recognize and appreciate the specific abilities You've entrusted to me. Give me clarity to see how these gifts can be used for Your glory and the benefit of others.

Lord, when I'm tempted to compare my gifts to others or doubt their value, remind me of Your purposeful design. Help me to embrace my uniqueness and to use my gifts with confidence and joy. May the recognition of my gifts lead to gratitude and faithful stewardship. In Jesus' name, Amen.

What unique gift has God given you that you can celebrate and use today?

Day 240: USE YOUR TALENTS TO GLORIFY GOD

"Each of you should use whatever gift you have received to serve others,
as faithful stewards of God's grace in its various forms."
(1 Peter 4:10, NIV)

Generous Father, thank You for the talents You've bestowed upon me. Help me to use these gifts faithfully to serve others and bring glory to Your name. Guide me in finding ways to employ my abilities in building Your kingdom and blessing those around me.

Lord, when I'm tempted to use my talents selfishly or to hide them out of fear, remind me of my responsibility as a steward of Your grace. May the use of my gifts be a testimony to Your goodness and an encouragement to others to discover and use their own talents. In Jesus' name, Amen.

How can you use one of your talents to serve others and glorify God today?

Day 241: DEVELOP YOUR ABILITIES

"Do you see someone skilled in their work? They will serve before kings;
they will not serve before officials of low rank"
(Proverbs 22:29, NIV)

Master Craftsman, thank You for the unique potential You've woven into my being. Grant me the diligence and perseverance to nurture the talents You've blessed me with. Help me to embrace my work with excellence, always eager to learn and improve.

Lord, surround me with a supportive community and mentors who can guide and inspire me. When challenges or setbacks arise, fill me with patience and determination. Let me view these obstacles as stepping stones for growth. May my abilities be a source of encouragement and help to those around me, reflecting Your love and purpose. Amen.

What specific step can you take today to further develop one of your abilities?

Day 242: OVERCOME INSECURITY

"For the Spirit God gave us does not make us timid,
but gives us power, love and self-discipline"
(2 Timothy 1:7, NIV)

Empowering God, I thank You for the spirit of power, love, and self-discipline You've given me. I am Your child, Your beloved. You have created me in Your image. Help me to overcome insecurities about my talents and abilities. Fill me with confidence rooted in Your love and purpose for my life.

Lord, when self-doubt or fear holds me back from using my gifts, remind me of Your strength working through me. Help me to step out boldly in faith, trusting that You will equip me for every good work You've prepared for me. May my confidence in You inspire others to overcome their own insecurities. In Jesus' name, Amen.

What insecurity about your talents do you need to surrender to God today?

*"You, my brothers and sisters, were called to be free. But do not use your freedom
to indulge the flesh; rather, serve one another humbly in love"*
(Galatians 5:13, NIV)

Lord, thank You for the freedom and talents You've blessed me with. I am grateful for the abilities You've entrusted to me, and I seek to use them for Your glory and the good of others. Help me to approach each day with a heart full of love and a spirit ready to serve.

Guide me to see the opportunities around me where I can make a difference. Teach me to act with humility and kindness, choosing to uplift others rather than seeking personal gain. When I am tempted to focus on myself, remind me of the joy and fulfillment that comes from serving others. In Jesus' name, Amen.

How can you use one of your talents to serve someone in need today?

Day 244: GOD'S PURPOSE FOR YOUR TALENTS

*"For we are God's handiwork, created in Christ Jesus to do good works,
which God prepared in advance for us to do"*
(Ephesians 2:10, NIV)

Heavenly Father, thank You for the special gifts and talents You've given me. I'm in awe of the unique way You've created me, and I want to use these abilities for the good things You have planned. Please guide me to see Your purpose in my talents and help me understand how to align my actions with Your will. Give me the courage and strength to follow Your path, even when I'm not sure where it leads.

Lord, keep my heart open to Your direction and my hands ready to help others. May my life be a reflection of Your love and handiwork, spreading kindness and light to everyone I meet. In Jesus' name, Amen.

**How can you align the use of your talents more
closely with God's purpose today?**

"Every good and perfect gift is from above, coming down from the Father
of the heavenly lights, who does not change like shifting shadows"
(James 1:17, NIV)

Generous Father, I thank You for every good and perfect gift You've given me, including my talents and abilities. Help me to cultivate a heart of gratitude for these gifts, recognizing that they come from Your unchanging goodness.

Lord, when I'm tempted to take credit for my abilities or to complain about the talents I lack, redirect my focus to Your generosity. Help me to use my gifts with thankfulness, always acknowledging You as the source. May my grateful heart be evident in how I steward and share the abilities You've given me. In Jesus' name, Amen.

How can you express gratitude to God for your talents in a tangible way today?

September

Week 36. Seeking God's Guidance in Parenting

Day 246: PRAY FOR WISDOM IN PARENTING

"If any of you lacks wisdom, you should ask God, who gives generously
to all without finding fault, and it will be given to you"
(James 1:5, NIV)

Heavenly Father, as a mother, I often feel overwhelmed by the responsibility of raising my children. I come before You, acknowledging my need for Your divine wisdom. Thank You for Your promise to give generously when I ask. Pour out Your wisdom upon me, Lord, that I may guide my children with grace and understanding.

Lord, grant me discernment to make decisions that align with Your will for my family. Help me to be patient when challenges arise and to seek Your counsel in every aspect of parenting. Amen.

What specific parenting challenge are you facing today?

"In everything set them an example by doing what is good."
(Titus 2:7, NIV)

Lord Jesus, You are the perfect example of goodness and love. As I strive to be a godly mother, help me to emulate Your character in all I do. I recognize that my children are watching and learning from my actions. Grant me the strength and courage to lead by example, even when it's difficult.

Father, guide my steps and guard my heart. May my life reflect Your love, kindness, and integrity. When I falter, give me the humility to acknowledge my mistakes and the wisdom to use them as teaching moments. Let my example inspire my children to seek You and live lives that honor You. Amen.

**In what area of your life do you need God's help
to set a better example for your children?**

Day 248: NURTURE CHILDREN'S FAITH

*"These commandments that I give you today are to be on your hearts.
Impress them on your children"*
(Deuteronomy 6:6-7, NIV)

Gracious God, I thank You for the privilege of nurturing my children's faith. Your Word is a lamp to our feet and a light to our path. Help me to first embrace Your commandments in my own heart, so that I may authentically share them with my children.

Lord, grant me creativity and patience as I teach Your truths. May our home be filled with Your presence, and may our conversations naturally turn to You. Give me discernment to recognize teachable moments and the words to explain Your love in ways my children can understand. Let their faith grow strong and deep, rooted in Your unchanging Word. Amen.

**What new way can you incorporate God's Word
into your family's daily routine this week?**

*"Fathers, do not exasperate your children; instead,
bring them up in the training and instruction of the Lord"
(Ephesians 6:4, NIV)*

Loving Father, I come to You seeking guidance in disciplining my children. Grant me Your patience and gentleness, that I may correct without exasperating. Help me to see beyond misbehavior to the hearts of my children, addressing their needs with Your compassion.

Lord, give me wisdom to establish boundaries that protect and nurture. When correction is necessary, let it be done in love, pointing always to Your grace. May my discipline reflect Your perfect balance of justice and mercy. Help me to instruct my children in Your ways, fostering in them a desire to honor You with their lives. Amen.

**How can you adjust your approach to discipline
to better reflect God's love and instruction?**

Day 250: CHILDREN'S PROTECTION

*"The Lord will keep you from all harm— he will watch over your life"
(Psalm 121:7, NIV)*

Almighty God, I lift my children up to You, trusting in Your promise of protection. In a world full of dangers seen and unseen, I find comfort in knowing that You watch over them. Surround them with Your hedge of protection, guarding their bodies, minds, and spirits.

Father, when I cannot be with them, I trust that You are. Give them wisdom to make safe choices and the courage to stand firm in their faith. When fears for their safety overwhelm me, remind me of Your constant presence and care. May Your protection be a testimony of Your love in their lives. Amen.

**How can you actively entrust your worries
about your children's safety to God today?**

"Trust in the Lord with all your heart and lean not on your own understanding"
(Proverbs 3:5, NIV)

Faithful God, I desire for my children to know the peace and security of trusting in You completely. Help me to model this trust in my own life, especially when circumstances are challenging. Guide me as I teach them to rely on You rather than their own understanding.

Lord, create opportunities for my children to experience Your faithfulness firsthand. When they face doubts or fears, remind them of Your unchanging love and power. May their trust in You grow deeper with each passing day. Grant me the words to explain Your trustworthiness in ways that resonate with their young hearts. Amen.

What personal story of God's faithfulness can you share
with your children to encourage their trust in Him?

Day 252: CULTIVATE A LOVING HOME ENVIRONMENT

"Love is patient, love is kind. It does not envy, it does not boast, it is not proud"
(1 Corinthians 13:4, NIV)

Heavenly Father, Your love is the perfect example for our family. Help me to cultivate a home environment that reflects Your patience and kind love. When tensions rise, or conflicts emerge, remind me to respond with the gentleness and humility that come from You.

Lord, fill our home with Your presence. May our words build up and encourage one another. Give me the strength to love selflessly, even when it's difficult. Help each family member to feel valued and cherished. Let the love we share within our home overflow to others, testifying to Your transforming power in our lives. Amen.

What specific action can you take today to make
your home a more loving and patient place?

Day 253: EMBRACE GOD'S FORGIVENESS

"If we confess our sins, he is faithful and just and will forgive
us our sins and purify us from all unrighteousness"
(1 John 1:9, NIV)

Merciful Father, I come before You with a humble heart, acknowledging my sins and shortcomings. Thank You for Your promise of forgiveness and cleansing. Help me to fully embrace the depth of Your grace and to live in the freedom it provides.

When guilt and shame threaten to overwhelm me, remind me of Your unfailing love and the power of Your forgiveness. Grant me the courage to confess my sins openly to You, trusting in Your faithfulness to purify and restore me. Amen.

How can you practically remind yourself of God's forgiveness
when you feel weighed down by past mistakes?

Day 254: EXTEND FORGIVENESS TO OTHERS

"Bear with each other and forgive one another if any of you has
a grievance against someone. Forgive as the Lord forgave you"
(Colossians 3:13, NIV)

Gracious God, You have shown me immeasurable forgiveness through Christ. Help me to extend that same forgiveness to others, even when it's difficult. Give me the strength to let go of grudges and grievances, and to see others through Your eyes of compassion.

When I struggle to forgive, remind me of the depth of Your forgiveness towards me. Soften my heart and help me to bear with others in love. Guide me in rebuilding relationships that have been damaged by unforgiveness. Amen.

Is there someone in your life you need to forgive?
What step can you take today towards extending that forgiveness?

"Get rid of all bitterness, rage and anger, brawling and slander,
along with every form of malice"
(Ephesians 4:31, NIV)

Heavenly Father, I confess that I sometimes hold onto bitterness and resentment. Your Word calls me to release these negative emotions, but I often find it challenging. Please give me the strength to let go of anger and malice. Help me to recognize when these feelings begin to take root in my heart.

Replace my bitterness with Your peace, my rage with Your calm, and my anger with Your love. Teach me to respond to hurt and disappointment in ways that honor You. May Your Spirit work in me to cultivate a heart of kindness and compassion instead of harboring ill feelings. Amen.

What specific bitterness or resentment do you need to release to God today?

Day 256: SEEK RECONCILIATION

"If it is possible, as far as it depends on you, live at peace with everyone"
(Romans 12:18, NIV)

Prince of Peace, I thank You for the reconciliation You've made possible between us and You. Help me to be an agent of reconciliation in my relationships. Give me the humility and courage to take the first step toward restoring broken relationships, even when it's uncomfortable.

Grant me wisdom to know how to approach difficult situations and the right words to speak. Where reconciliation seems impossible, remind me that with You, all things are possible. Help me to do my part in living at peace with others, trusting You with the outcomes. May my efforts at reconciliation reflect Your heart for unity and peace. Amen.

Is there a relationship in your life that needs reconciliation?
What can you do this week to work towards peace in that relationship?

Day 257: FORGIVE REPEATEDLY

"Then Peter came to Jesus and asked, 'Lord, how many times shall I forgive my brother or sister who sins against me? Up to seven times?' Jesus answered, 'I tell you, not seven times, but seventy-seven times'"
(Matthew 18:21-22, NIV)

Lord Jesus, Your teaching on forgiveness challenges me. It's often difficult to forgive once, let alone repeatedly. Yet You call me to a higher standard of forgiveness, reflecting Your own limitless grace. Help me to cultivate a heart that is always ready to forgive.

When I'm tempted to keep count of others' wrongs, remind me of the countless times You've forgiven me. Give me the strength to choose forgiveness over resentment, time and time again. May Your endless mercy flow through me, transforming my relationships and bringing healing where there has been hurt. Amen.

**How can you cultivate a habit of readiness to
forgive in your daily interactions with others?**

Day 258: PRAY FOR THOSE WHO HURT YOU

"But I tell you, love your enemies and pray for those who persecute you"
(Matthew 5:44, NIV)

Loving Father, Your command to pray for those who hurt me is one of the most challenging aspects of following You. It goes against my natural instincts. Yet I know that You call me to a supernatural love. Give me the grace to pray sincerely for those who have caused me pain.

Help me to see them as You see them – as individuals in need of Your love and grace, just as I am. Soften my heart towards them and replace any desire for revenge with genuine concern for their well-being. Amen.

**Who is someone who has hurt you that you need to start praying for?
How can you begin to pray for their good?**

*"Do not take revenge, my dear friends, but leave room for God's wrath,
for it is written: 'It is mine to avenge; I will repay,' says the Lord."*
(Romans 12:19, NIV)

Righteous God, when I've been wronged, it's tempting to seek revenge or to demand immediate justice. Help me to resist this urge and to trust in Your perfect justice. Give me the faith to leave room for Your wrath, knowing that You see all and will address all wrongs in Your time and way.

Grant me patience when justice seems delayed, and help me to release my desire for vengeance into Your capable hands. Fill me with Your peace, even in the face of injustice. May my trust in Your justice free me from bitterness and allow me to extend grace to others. Amen.

**In what situation do you need to trust God's
justice rather than seeking your own revenge?**

Week 38. Embracing Biblical Womanhood

Day 260: RECOGNIZE YOUR WORTH IN CHRIST

"She is clothed with strength and dignity; she can laugh at the days to come"
(Proverbs 31:25, NIV)

Heavenly Father, thank You for clothing me with strength and dignity through Christ. Help me to fully embrace the worth You've bestowed upon me as Your daughter. When doubts creep in, remind me that my value comes not from worldly standards, but from Your unfailing love. Grant me the confidence to face the future with joy.

May Your strength be evident in my life, allowing me to stand firm in my faith and to inspire others. Help me to walk in the assurance of Your love, laughing at the days to come because I trust in Your sovereign care. Amen.

**How can you remind yourself of your worth in
Christ when you face moments of self-doubt?**

"Your beauty should not come from outward adornment, such as elaborate hairstyles and the wearing of gold jewelry or fine clothes. Rather, it should be that of your inner self, the unfading beauty of a gentle and quiet spirit, which is of great worth in God's sight"
(1 Peter 3:3-4, NIV)

Lord, in a world that often prioritizes outward appearance, help me to focus on cultivating inner beauty. Remind me that while external beauty fades, the beauty of a gentle and quiet spirit is timeless and precious to You. Teach me to nurture qualities that reflect Your character - kindness, patience, and love.

When I'm tempted to find my worth in my appearance, redirect my heart to the unfading beauty of a spirit aligned with Yours. May my life be adorned with good deeds and a heart that seeks after You. Let my inner beauty shine through, drawing others to the source of true beauty - Your transforming love. Amen.

What is one way you can invest in your inner beauty today?

Day 262: SEEK GODLY WISDOM

"Charm is deceptive, and beauty is fleeting;
but a woman who fears the Lord is to be praised"
(Proverbs 31:30, NIV)

Wise and loving God, I come before You seeking the wisdom that comes from knowing and revering You. Help me to prioritize my relationship with You above all else, recognizing that true fulfillment comes from fearing You. When I'm tempted to rely on charm or physical beauty, remind me of their fleeting nature. Instead, cultivate in me a heart that seeks after Your wisdom and truth.

Grant me discernment in my daily decisions and the courage to live according to Your principles. Let my actions and words reflect the wisdom that comes from above. Amen.

In what area of your life do you most need to seek God's wisdom right now?

"For we are God's handiwork, created in Christ Jesus to do good works,
which God prepared in advance for us to do"
(Ephesians 2:10, NIV)

Creator God, thank You for making me Your unique handiwork. Help me to embrace the special calling You've placed on my life. When I'm tempted to compare myself to others or doubt my purpose, remind me that You've created me with intention and love.

Give me clarity to recognize the good works You've prepared for me and the courage to step into them confidently. Help me to see my life as a canvas for Your artistry, and to cooperate with Your Spirit as You work in and through me. Let me find joy and fulfillment in living out the purpose for which You created me. Amen.

What unique gifts or talents has God given you,
and how can you use them to serve others this week?

Day 264: NURTURE RELATIONSHIPS

"Two are better than one, because they have a good return for their labor"
(Ecclesiastes 4:9, NIV)

Loving Father, thank You for the gift of relationships. Help me to nurture and value the connections You've placed in my life. Give me wisdom to invest in friendships that encourage and strengthen my faith. When relationships become challenging, grant me patience, understanding, and the willingness to extend grace.

Help me to be a faithful friend, offering support and companionship to those around me. Let me be a source of encouragement and positivity in my interactions with others. Guide me in building and maintaining healthy, God-centered relationships that bear good fruit in my life and in the lives of those around me. Amen.

How can you intentionally nurture an important
relationship in your life this week?

"Serve wholeheartedly, as if you were serving the Lord, not people"
(Ephesians 6:7, NIV)

Gracious God, thank You for the opportunity to serve others as an expression of my love for You. Help me to approach every task, no matter how mundane, with a joyful and willing heart. When serving becomes difficult or thankless, remind me that my ultimate audience is You. Fill me with Your love so that it overflows in my service to others.

May my attitude in serving reflect Your character and draw others to You. Help me to see each opportunity to serve as a chance to worship You and to make Your love tangible to those around me. Let my service be a testament to Your grace working in my life. Amen.

**In what area of your life do you need to
cultivate a more joyful attitude in serving?**

Day 266: TRUST GOD'S PLAN FOR YOUR LIFE

*"For I know the plans I have for you,' declares the Lord, 'plans to prosper
you and not to harm you, plans to give you hope and a future'"*
(Jeremiah 29:11, NIV)

Sovereign Lord, I thank You for Your promise of good plans for my life. Help me to trust in Your perfect timing and purposes, even when I can't see or understand them. When uncertainty or fear about the future creeps in, remind me of Your faithfulness and Your promise to give me hope and a future.

Give me the patience to wait on Your timing and wisdom to recognize Your guidance. Help me to walk confidently in the path You've set before me, trusting that Your plans for me are far better than anything I could devise for myself. Let my life be a testimony to Your goodness and Your perfect plan. Amen.

What area of your life do you need to surrender to God's plan today?

Day 267: TRUST GOD AS THE ULTIMATE HEALER

"Praise the Lord, my soul, and forget not all his benefits—
who forgives all your sins and heals all your diseases"
(Psalm 103:2-3, NIV)

Loving Father, I come before You today, recognizing You as the ultimate healer of both body and soul. Thank You for Your countless benefits, especially the forgiveness of my sins and Your healing power. Grant me the faith to believe in Your healing power, even when my circumstances seem unchanging.

May I never take Your benefits for granted. Whether You choose to heal me immediately or to walk with me through a longer journey of recovery, help me to trust Your timing and Your methods. Let my experience of Your healing touch draw me closer to You and be a testimony of Your love to others. Amen.

How can you cultivate a deeper trust in God's healing power in your life today?

Day 268: SEEK EMOTIONAL WHOLENESS

"The Lord is close to the brokenhearted and saves those who are crushed in spirit"
(Psalm 34:18, NIV)

Compassionate God, I thank You for Your promise to be near to the brokenhearted. In moments when my spirit feels crushed, draw me close to Your comforting presence. Help me to bring all my emotional pain and wounds to You, trusting in Your gentle healing touch.

When I feel overwhelmed by sadness, anxiety, or hurt, remind me that You are right there with me, ready to save and restore. Let Your love fill the broken places in my heart. Use my journey towards emotional health to make me more compassionate towards others who are hurting. Amen.

What emotional burden do you need to bring to God for healing today?

"Do you not know that your bodies are temples of the Holy Spirit, who is in you,
whom you have received from God? You are not your own."
(1 Corinthians 6:19, NIV)

Holy Spirit, thank You for making Your home in me. Help me to honor You by caring well for this body You've entrusted to me. Give me wisdom and discipline to make healthy choices in my diet, exercise, and rest. When I'm tempted to neglect my health or indulge in unhealthy habits, remind me that my body is Your temple.

Grant me the strength to break free from any behaviors that don't align with Your best for me. Help me to see caring for my body as an act of worship and stewardship. Let my commitment to a healthy lifestyle be a testament to Your transforming work in me and an example to others. Amen.

What is one healthy habit you can start or improve
upon this week to honor God with your body?

Day 270: FIND STRENGTH IN WEAKNESS

"That is why, for Christ's sake, I delight in weaknesses, in insults, in hardships,
in persecutions, in difficulties. For when I am weak, then I am strong"
(2 Corinthians 12:10, NIV)

Mighty God, I confess that it's often difficult for me to delight in my weaknesses. Yet Your Word teaches me that it's in my weakness that Your strength is perfected. Help me to embrace my limitations and struggles, knowing that they create space for Your power to be displayed in my life.

When I face hardships, insults, or difficulties, remind me that these are opportunities for Your strength to shine through me. Give me the faith to boast in my weaknesses. Amen.

In what area of weakness do you need to invite God's strength today?

"For God has not given us a spirit of fear, but of power and of love and of a sound mind"
(2 Timothy 1:7, NKJV)

Gracious Father, I thank You for the promise of a sound mind. In moments when my thoughts feel clouded by fear or confusion, remind me that You've given me a spirit of power, love, and self-discipline. Help me to take captive every thought that doesn't align with Your truth.

Give me discernment to recognize lies and replace them with Your truth. May Your Word be a lamp to my feet, illuminating my path and bringing clarity to my decisions. Help me to cultivate habits that promote mental health and to seek help when I need it. Let my mind be renewed daily by Your Spirit, transforming me more into the likeness of Christ. Amen.

**What practical steps can you take today to
cultivate greater mental clarity and peace?**

Day 272: EMBRACE GOD'S PEACE

"Do not be anxious about anything, but in every situation, by prayer and petition, with thanksgiving, present your requests to God. And the peace of God, which transcends all understanding, will guard your hearts and your minds in Christ Jesus"
(Philippians 4:6-7, NIV)

Prince of Peace, I come before You with all my anxieties and concerns. Thank You for inviting me to bring everything to You in prayer. Help me to cultivate a habit of turning to You first in every situation, big or small. When worry creeps in, remind me to present my requests to You with thanksgiving, trusting in Your faithfulness.

May this supernatural peace guard my heart and mind, keeping out fear and doubt. Teach me to rest in Your presence. Thank You for the assurance that Your peace is always available to me in Christ Jesus. Amen.

What specific anxiety do you need to surrender to God today?

Day 273: SEEK HOLISTIC WELL-BEING

"Dear friend, I pray that you may enjoy good health and that all
may go well with you, even as your soul is getting along well"
(3 John 1:2, NIV)

Loving God, I thank You for Your desire to see me thrive in every area of my life - body, mind, and spirit. Help me to pursue holistic well-being, recognizing that all aspects of my health are interconnected. Guide me in making choices that promote physical health, emotional balance, and spiritual growth. When I'm tempted to neglect one area of my well-being, remind me of the importance of caring for my whole self.

Lord, please grant me wisdom to recognize areas where I need to grow or seek help. Help me to steward well the life You've given me, honoring You in body, mind, and spirit. Amen.

What area of your holistic well-being (physical, emotional, spiritual)
needs the most attention right now, and how can you address it?

October

Week 40. Growing in Spiritual Disciplines

Day 274: CULTIVATE A HABIT OF PRAYER

"Devote yourselves to prayer, being watchful and thankful."
(Colossians 4:2, NIV)

Heavenly Father, I come before You with a desire to deepen my prayer life. Help me to cultivate a habit of consistent, heartfelt prayer. Teach me to be watchful, recognizing Your work in my life and the needs of those around me.

Fill my heart with gratitude, that thanksgiving may flavor all my prayers. When distractions come, or my motivation wanes, remind me of the privilege and power of communing with You. Let my prayer life draw me closer to Your heart and align my will with Yours. Amen.

What practical steps can you take to make prayer
a more consistent part of your daily routine?

"Do your best to present yourself to God as one approved, a worker who does not need to be ashamed and who correctly handles the word of truth"
(2 Timothy 2:15, NIV)

Lord of Truth, I thank You for the gift of Your Word. Instill in me a deep hunger for Scripture and the discipline to study it regularly. Help me to approach Your Word not just as a task to complete, but as a way to know You more intimately. Grant me the wisdom to see how Scripture applies to my daily life and decisions.

May Your Word shape my thoughts, guide my actions, and mold my character. Use my study of Scripture to equip me for every good work You've prepared for me. Amen.

**What specific plan can you implement to make
regular Bible study a priority in your life?**

Day 276: PRACTICE FASTING

"When you fast, do not look somber as the hypocrites do, for they disfigure their faces to show others they are fasting. Truly I tell you, they have received their reward in full"
(Matthew 6:16, NIV)

Gracious God, as I consider the discipline of fasting, I ask for Your guidance and strength. Help me to approach fasting not as a way to impress others or earn Your favor, but as a means to draw closer to You and align my heart with Yours.

When I fast, remind me to do so with a joyful heart, knowing that You see what is done in secret. Give me wisdom to choose appropriate times and methods for fasting. Please heighten my spiritual sensitivity and deepen my dependence on You. Use this discipline to reveal areas in my life where I need to grow or change. Amen.

**What form of fasting might God be calling you
to practice, and for what spiritual purpose?**

"Let the message of Christ dwell among you richly as you teach and admonish one another with all wisdom through psalms, hymns, and songs from the Spirit, singing to God with gratitude in your hearts"
(Colossians 3:16, NIV)

Lord of all creation, I come before You with a heart ready to worship. Help me to engage in worship not just during church services, but as a way of life. May the message of Christ dwell richly in me, overflowing into songs of praise and thanksgiving. Give me a new song to sing to You each day, whether in times of joy or sorrow.

When I'm tempted to let the cares of this world dampen my worship, remind me of Your worthiness and faithfulness. Let my life be a living sacrifice, holy and pleasing to You. Use times of corporate worship to encourage and build up my faith and the faith of others. Amen.

How can you incorporate more genuine worship into your daily life this week?

Day 278: SERVE OTHERS

"Each of you should use whatever gift you have received to serve others, as faithful stewards of God's grace in its various forms."
(1 Peter 4:10, NIV)

Generous Father, thank You for the gifts and abilities You've given me. Help me to recognize these gifts and use them faithfully to serve others. Give me eyes to see the needs around me and a willing heart to meet them. When serving becomes challenging or thankless, remind me that I'm ultimately serving You.

Help me to serve with humility, not seeking recognition but desiring only to glorify You. Show me creative ways to use my unique talents and resources to bless others and advance Your kingdom. Amen.

**What specific gift or ability has God given you
that you can use to serve others this week?**

*"Be still, and know that I am God; I will be exalted
among the nations, I will be exalted in the earth"*
(Psalm 46:10, NIV)

Prince of Peace, in the midst of this noisy and busy world, I come seeking the quiet of Your presence. Teach me the value of solitude and silence. Help me to carve out regular times to be still before You, quieting my heart and mind to listen for Your voice.

When I'm tempted to fill every moment with activity or noise, remind me of my need for silent reflection and communion with You. In moments of solitude, reveal to me the areas of my life that need Your touch. Let the peace I find in these moments overflow into every area of my life, making me a calming presence to those around me. Amen.

**How can you create space for solitude and
silence in your daily routine this week?**

Day 280: CULTIVATE SPIRITUAL FELLOWSHIP

*"And let us consider how we may spur one another on toward love and good deeds,
not giving up meeting together, as some are in the habit of doing, but encouraging
one another—and all the more as you see the Day approaching"*
(Hebrews 10:24-25, NIV)

Loving God, thank You for the gift of the Christian community. Help me to prioritize spiritual fellowship in my life, recognizing its importance for my growth and encouragement. Give me the courage to be vulnerable with trusted believers, sharing both my joys and struggles. When I'm tempted to isolate myself, remind me of my need for the support and accountability of other Christians.

Help me to be an encouragement to others, spurring them on toward love and good deeds. Use our fellowship to sharpen me spiritually and to prepare me for Your return. Amen.

What steps can you take to deepen your involvement in spiritual fellowship?

Day 281: REMEMBER GOD'S PAST FAITHFULNESS

"I will remember the deeds of the Lord; yes, I will remember your miracles of long ago"
(Psalm 77:11, NIV)

Faithful God, today I pause to remember Your countless acts of faithfulness in my life. Thank You for the miracles, both great and small, that You've performed. Help me to recall Your provision, protection, and guidance throughout my journey.

When doubts creep in, or challenges loom large, remind me of the ways You've come through for me in the past. May the memory of Your faithfulness strengthen my trust in You for today and tomorrow. Give me the wisdom to share these stories of Your goodness with others, that they, too, may be encouraged. Amen.

**What specific act of God's faithfulness in your
past can you reflect on and thank Him for today?**

Day 282: TRUST GOD'S PRESENT FAITHFULNESS

*"Because of the Lord's great love we are not consumed, for his compassions
never fail. They are new every morning; great is your faithfulness"*
(Lamentations 3:22-23, NIV)

Compassionate Father, I thank You for Your faithfulness that is new every morning. Help me to trust in Your unfailing love and mercy for this day. When I'm tempted to worry about my current circumstances, remind me that Your compassions never fail. Give me eyes to see Your faithfulness at work in my life right now, even in the midst of challenges or uncertainty.

Help me to approach each day with the expectation of experiencing Your fresh mercies. Thank You for Your love that sustains me and keeps me from being consumed by life's difficulties. Amen.

How can you actively look for God's faithfulness in your life?

*"Being confident of this, that he who began a good work in you
will carry it on to completion until the day of Christ Jesus"
(Philippians 1:6, NIV)*

Sovereign Lord, I thank You for the assurance that You will complete the good work You've begun in me. Help me to look to the future with hope and confidence, trusting in Your unwavering faithfulness. When I'm discouraged by my slow progress or setbacks, remind me that You are not finished with me yet.

Lord, please help me live each day in light of eternity, knowing that You are faithfully preparing me for Your purposes. Let this confidence in Your future faithfulness motivate me to persevere in faith and good works. Thank You for the promise that You will see Your work in me through to completion. Amen.

What area of your life do you need to entrust to God's future faithfulness?

Day 284: GOD'S FAITHFULNESS IN TRIALS

*"Consider it pure joy, my brothers and sisters, whenever you face trials of many kinds,
because you know that the testing of your faith produces perseverance"
(James 1:2-3, NIV)*

Loving Father, I confess that it's often difficult to find joy in trials. Yet I thank You for Your faithfulness that sustains me through every challenge. Help me to see my trials through Your eyes, recognizing them as opportunities for growth and deepened faith.

When I'm tempted to despair in difficult times, remind me of Your presence and Your purpose at work in my life. Give me the strength to persevere and the wisdom to learn the lessons You have for me in each trial. Amen.

How can you choose to see God's faithfulness in a current trial you're facing?

"Come and hear, all you who fear God; let me tell you what he has done for me"
(Psalm 66:16, NIV)

Gracious God, thank You for all the ways You've demonstrated Your faithfulness in my life. Give me courage and opportunities to share these testimonies with others. Help me to overcome any hesitation or fear when speaking about Your goodness.

Give me wisdom to know which experiences to share and how to communicate them effectively. Let my testimonies point others to You as the source of all goodness and faithfulness. Use my words to strengthen the faith of fellow believers and to draw those who don't know You closer to Your love. Thank You for the privilege of being a witness to Your ongoing work in the world. Amen.

**What specific testimony of God's faithfulness in
your life can you share with someone this week?**

Day 286: REST IN GOD'S UNCHANGING NATURE

"Jesus Christ is the same yesterday and today and forever"
(Hebrews 13:8, NIV)

Immutable God, I thank You that You never change. In a world of constant flux and uncertainty, You remain steadfast and true. Help me to find deep rest and security in Your unchanging nature. When everything around me seems unstable, remind me that You are my rock and my fortress.

Your purposes remain the same, regardless of my circumstances. Let the unchanging nature of Jesus Christ fill me with confidence to face whatever changes come my way. Help me to align my life with Your eternal truths rather than the shifting values of this world. Thank You for being a God I can always rely on, no matter what. Amen.

**How can meditating on God's unchanging nature bring
you comfort and stability in your current situation?**

*"I will sing of the Lord's great love forever; with my mouth I
will make your faithfulness known through all generations"*
(Psalm 89:1, NIV)

Faithful God, my heart overflows with praise for Your unwavering faithfulness. Thank You for Your great love that endures forever. Help me to make Your faithfulness known through my words and actions. When I'm tempted to complain or doubt, turn my heart toward praise instead. Give me a song of joy to sing, celebrating Your constant care and provision.

Let praise for Your faithfulness be ever on my lips, in good times and in challenging ones. Use my witness to draw others into a deeper appreciation of Your steadfast love. Thank You for being faithful even when I am faithless. Amen.

In what creative way can you express your praise for God's faithfulness today?

Week 42. Clinging to God's Promises

Day 288: TRUST GOD'S PROMISES OF SALVATION

*"For God so loved the world that he gave his one and only Son,
that whoever believes in him shall not perish but have eternal life."*
(John 3:16, NIV)

Loving Father, I am in awe of Your incredible love for me and for all of humanity. Thank You for the precious gift of Your Son, Jesus Christ, and for the promise of eternal life through Him. Help me to fully grasp the depth of Your love and the magnitude of this promise of salvation.

When doubts creep in, or I feel unworthy, remind me that Your gift is freely given to all who believe. Strengthen my faith in this promise, allowing it to transform how I live each day. Help me to live in light of this amazing promise, fully embracing the abundant life You offer. Amen.

**How can you live today in a way that reflects
your trust in God's promise of salvation?**

"And my God will meet all your needs according to the riches of his glory in Christ Jesus"
(Philippians 4:19, NIV)

Jehovah Jireh, my Provider, I thank You for Your promise to meet all my needs. Help me to trust in Your provision, especially when circumstances seem uncertain or resources appear scarce. Remind me that Your riches in glory are limitless and that You care deeply about every aspect of my life.

When I'm tempted to worry about my needs, turn my heart to gratitude for all the ways You've provided in the past. Give me wisdom to distinguish between my wants and my true needs, trusting You to supply what is best for me. Thank You for the assurance that in Christ, I lack nothing truly necessary for life and godliness. Amen.

**What specific need can you entrust to God today,
relying on His promise of provision?**

Day 290: EMBRACE GOD'S PROMISE OF PEACE

"Peace I leave with you; my peace I give you. I do not give to you as the world gives.
Do not let your hearts be troubled and do not be afraid"
(John 14:27, NIV)

Prince of Peace, I come to You seeking the peace that only You can give. Thank You for Your promise of a peace that surpasses all understanding. In the midst of life's storms and uncertainties, help me to embrace and hold onto Your perfect peace. When anxiety threatens to overwhelm me, remind me of Your presence and Your power to calm every storm.

May Your peace guard my heart and mind, allowing me to face each day with confidence and trust in You. Let Your peace be evident in my life, drawing others to the source of true serenity. Amen.

**How can you actively choose to embrace God's
peace in a challenging situation you're facing?**

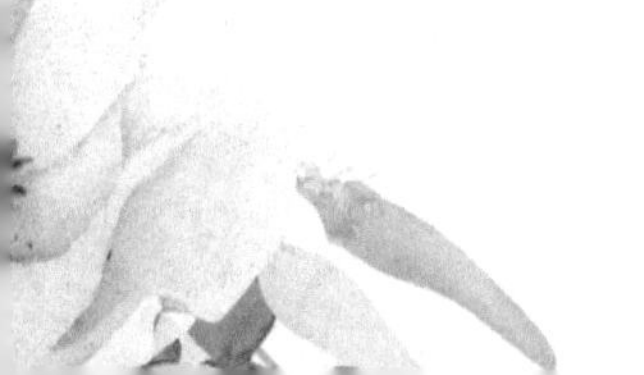

"But those who hope in the Lord will renew their strength. They will soar on wings like eagles; they will run and not grow weary, they will walk and not be faint"
(Isaiah 40:31, NIV)

Almighty God, I thank You for Your promise to renew my strength as I hope in You. In moments of weakness and weariness, help me to hold firmly to this promise. Remind me that Your strength is made perfect in my weakness. When I feel unable to face the challenges before me, lift me up on wings like eagles. Give me the endurance to run the race You've set before me without growing weary.

In the daily walk of faith, sustain me so that I do not faint. May my reliance on Your strength be a witness to others of Your power at work in my life. Let me find rest and renewal in Your presence each day. Help me to soar above my circumstances, carried by Your mighty power. Amen.

In what area of your life do you most need to
experience God's renewing strength today?

Day 292: GOD'S PROMISE OF FORGIVENESS

"If we confess our sins, he is faithful and just and will forgive us our sins and purify us from all unrighteousness"
(1 John 1:9, NIV)

Merciful Father, I come before You, grateful for Your promise of forgiveness. Thank You for Your faithfulness and justice that ensure my sins are forgiven when I confess them to You. Help me to approach You with honesty and humility, acknowledging my faults and failures.

Give me the courage to confess my sins fully, trusting in Your promise to cleanse me from all unrighteousness. May the reality of Your forgiveness free me to live in the joy of Your presence. Help me to extend this same forgiveness to others, reflecting the grace I've received. Amen.

Is there a sin you need to confess to God today,
trusting in His promise of forgiveness?

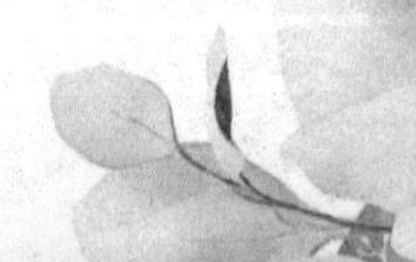

*"Trust in the Lord with all your heart and lean not on your own understanding;
in all your ways submit to him, and he will make your paths straight"*
(Proverbs 3:5-6, NIV)

Wise and loving God, I thank You for Your promise to guide me through life. Help me to trust You completely, especially when Your ways don't align with my own understanding. Give me the humility to submit all my plans and decisions to You, confident that You will direct my paths.

May Your Holy Spirit illuminate the way I should go, making my paths straight before me. Let my life be characterized by a deep trust in Your leadership, inspiring others to seek Your guidance as well. Thank You for Your perfect knowledge of my future and Your promise to lead me in the best way. Amen.

**What decision or area of your life do you need
to fully submit to God's guidance today?**

Day 294: GOD'S PROMISE OF ETERNAL LIFE

"And this is the testimony: God has given us eternal life, and this life is in his Son"
(1 John 5:11, NIV)

Eternal God, I am overwhelmed with gratitude for Your promise of eternal life through Your Son, Jesus Christ. Help me to hold fast to this promise, allowing it to shape my perspective on both this life and the life to come. When the cares of this world threaten to distract me, remind me of my eternal destiny in You.

Give me the courage to live boldly for You, knowing that my true life is hidden with Christ in God. Let the promise of eternity motivate me to invest in things of lasting value and to share this good news with others. Help me to live each day in light of eternity, eagerly anticipating the day when I will see You face to face. Amen.

**How can the promise of eternal life impact the way
you approach your daily life and decisions?**

Day 295: CULTIVATE COMPASSION FOR THE POOR

"Whoever is kind to the poor lends to the Lord,
and he will reward them for what they have done"
(Proverbs 19:17, NIV)

Compassionate Father, open my eyes and my heart to the needs of the poor around me. Help me to see them as You see them - precious individuals made in Your image. When I'm tempted to judge or ignore those in poverty, remind me that in serving them, I'm lending to You.

Help me know how to best help those in need. May my actions reflect Your love and bring hope to those struggling with poverty. Help me to use the resources You've given me to make a tangible difference in the lives of the poor. Amen.

What practical step can you take this week to
show kindness to someone living in poverty?

Day 296: SEEK JUSTICE FOR THE OPPRESSED

"Defend the weak and the fatherless; uphold the cause of the poor and the oppressed"
(Psalm 82:3, NIV)

God of Justice, I come before You on behalf of the oppressed and vulnerable in our world. Give me the courage and wisdom to defend those who cannot defend themselves. Open my eyes to the injustices around me and show me how I can be a voice for the voiceless. When I'm tempted to remain silent or look away, remind me of Your heart for justice.

Help me to uphold the cause of the poor and oppressed through my words, actions, and prayers. Guide me in using whatever influence I have to promote fairness and equity. May my efforts to seek justice reflect Your character and draw others to Your righteousness. Amen.

How can you actively seek justice for an oppressed
group in your community this week?

*"Is it not to share your food with the hungry and to provide the poor
wanderer with shelter— when you see the naked, to clothe them,
and not to turn away from your own flesh and blood?"*
(Isaiah 58:7, NIV)

Merciful God, my heart aches for those who have no place to call home. I lift up to You all those experiencing homelessness in my community and around the world. Provide them with shelter, safety, and the basic necessities of life. When I encounter someone who is homeless, help me to see them as You see them - with dignity and worth.

Give me the compassion to share what I have, whether it's food, clothing, or simply my time and attention. Thank You for the home and security You've provided me. Help me to never take these blessings for granted but to use them to bless others. Amen.

What tangible way can you help someone experiencing homelessness this week?

Day 298: INTERCEDE FOR THE SICK

*"Is anyone among you sick? Let them call the elders of the church to pray
over them and anoint them with oil in the name of the Lord."*
(James 5:14, NIV)

Healing God, I come before You on behalf of all those who are suffering from illness or disease. You know each one by name and understand their pain. I ask for Your healing touch in their lives - physically, emotionally, and spiritually. Give strength and comfort to those who are sick, and wisdom and skill to those caring for them.

When I encounter someone who is ill, help me to respond with compassion and to offer the support they need. Remind me of the power of intercessory prayer and guide me in praying effectively for the sick. May Your healing presence be felt in hospitals, homes, and wherever there is suffering. Amen.

Who can you specifically pray for today who is dealing with illness?

"Religion that God our Father accepts as pure and faultless is this: to look after orphans and widows in their distress and to keep oneself from being polluted by the world"
(James 1:27, NIV)

Heavenly Father, You are a defender of widows and a father to the fatherless. I lift up to You all those who have lost spouses or parents. Comfort them in their grief and provide for their needs. Show me how I can support and encourage widows and orphans in my community.

Give me a heart of compassion and the wisdom to know how to help practically. When I'm tempted to focus only on my own concerns, remind me of Your call to look after those in distress. May my actions reflect Your love and bring hope to those who feel alone or abandoned. Amen.

What specific action can you take this week to support a widow or orphan in your community?

Day 300: PRAY FOR THOSE IN PRISON

"Continue to remember those in prison as if you were together with them in prison, and those who are mistreated as if you yourselves were suffering"
(Hebrews 13:3, NIV)

Merciful God, I lift up to You all those who are incarcerated. You know their stories, their struggles, and their hearts. I ask for Your presence to be felt within prison walls, bringing hope, comfort, and transformation. Protect those who are vulnerable and guide those who are seeking rehabilitation.

When I think of those in prison, help me to see them as You see them - individuals worthy of love and second chances. Show me how I can support prison ministries or contribute to programs that aid in rehabilitation and reintegration. Amen.

How can you show support for someone affected by incarceration this week?

"Speak up for those who cannot speak for themselves,
for the rights of all who are destitute"
(Proverbs 31:8, NIV)

Righteous God, You call us to be a voice for the voiceless and to stand up for those who cannot stand up for themselves. Give me the courage and wisdom to advocate for the rights of the destitute and marginalized. Open my eyes to the injustices around me and show me how I can make a difference.

When I'm tempted to stay silent out of fear or apathy, remind me of Your heart for justice and Your call to speak up. Guide me in using my voice, my vote, and my influence to promote the well-being of those who are often overlooked or ignored. Amen.

**What issue affecting the voiceless or destitute can
you learn more about and speak up for this week?**

Week 44. Embracing Gratitude and Thanksgiving

Day 302: CULTIVATE A THANKFUL HEART

"Give thanks in all circumstances; for this is God's will for you in Christ Jesus"
(1 Thessalonians 5:18, NIV)

Gracious Father, I come before You today asking for Your help in cultivating a truly thankful heart. I confess that it's often easy to be grateful when things are going well, but much harder when I face challenges or disappointments. Help me to see Your goodness and faithfulness in every circumstance of my life.

When I'm tempted to complain, remind me of the many blessings You've poured into my life. Give me the strength and perspective to give thanks even in difficult times, trusting that You are working all things for my good. In Jesus' name, Amen.

What are three things you can thank God for right now?

"Every good and perfect gift is from above, coming down from the Father
of the heavenly lights, who does not change like shifting shadows"
(James 1:17, NIV)

Heavenly Father, I am overwhelmed by Your goodness and the many blessings You've poured into my life. Thank You for being the source of every good gift. Help me to recognize Your hand in both the big and small blessings of each day.

When I'm tempted to take Your gifts for granted or to claim credit for the good things in my life, remind me that all I have comes from You. Give me eyes to see the often-overlooked blessings - the beauty of creation, the gift of relationships, the provision of my daily needs. Thank You for Your faithfulness that never wavers, even when circumstances change. Amen.

Can you list five specific blessings in your life
that you want to express gratitude for today?

Day 304: THANK GOD FOR SALVATION

"But thanks be to God! He gives us the victory through our Lord Jesus Christ"
(1 Corinthians 15:57, NIV)

Merciful Savior, my heart overflows with gratitude for the gift of salvation You've given me through Jesus Christ. Thank You for the victory over sin and death that is mine because of Your sacrifice. Help me to live each day in the joy and freedom of this salvation, never taking it for granted. When I'm tempted to doubt Your love or to stray from Your path, remind me of the price You paid to redeem me.

Give me opportunities to share the good news of this salvation with others, that they, too, might know the victory found in Christ. Help me to walk worthy of the calling I've received, always giving thanks for Your indescribable gift. Amen.

How can you express your gratitude for salvation in a tangible way?

"The heavens declare the glory of God; the skies proclaim the work of his hands"
(Psalm 19:1, NIV)

Creator God, I stand in awe of the beauty and complexity of Your creation. Thank You for the wonders that surround me, from the vastness of the universe to the intricacy of a single flower. Help me to see Your handiwork in the world around me and to pause in appreciation of its beauty.

When I'm rushed or distracted, remind me to take time to observe and enjoy the natural world You've made. Give me a deeper understanding of my role as a steward of Your creation, guiding me in caring for the earth and its resources. Help me to join all of creation in declaring Your glory and praising Your name. Amen.

**What aspect of God's creation can you take
time to appreciate and thank Him for today?**

Day 306: BE GRATEFUL FOR TRIALS

*"Consider it pure joy, my brothers and sisters, whenever you face trials of many kinds,
because you know that the testing of your faith produces perseverance"*
(James 1:2–3, NIV)

Sovereign Lord, I confess that it's often difficult to be grateful in the midst of trials. Yet I thank You for the growth and perseverance that come through challenges. Help me to see my trials through Your eyes, recognizing them as opportunities for spiritual maturity.

Give me the strength to persevere and the wisdom to learn the lessons You have for me in each trial. May my response to challenges be a testimony to Your grace and faithfulness. Let the testing of my faith produce in me a steadfast character that honors You. Amen.

**Can you identify a current trial in your life and
find one aspect of it to be grateful for?**

"Give thanks to the Lord, for he is good; his love endures forever."
(Psalm 107:1, NIV)

Ever-present God, I thank You for Your constant presence in my life. Your goodness and love surround me every moment of every day. Help me to be more aware of Your presence, especially in the ordinary moments of life.

When I feel alone or forgotten, remind me that You are always with me, that Your love never fails. Give me a deeper appreciation for the comfort and strength I find in Your presence. Let my thankfulness for Your goodness overflow into praise and worship. Help me to live each day in the joy of Your presence, sharing that joy with those around me. Amen.

**How can you practice being more aware of
God's presence throughout your day today?**

Day 308: EXPRESS GRATITUDE FOR OTHERS

"I thank my God every time I remember you."
(Philippians 1:3, NIV)

Loving Father, I thank You for the gift of relationships and the people You've placed in my life. Help me to appreciate the unique value of each person and to express my gratitude for them. When I'm tempted to take others for granted or to focus on their faults, remind me of the positive impact they have on my life.

Lord, please give me opportunities to encourage and uplift those around me through words of gratitude and acts of kindness. Let my relationships be characterized by thankfulness, fostering deeper connections and mutual growth. Help me to be a source of joy and gratitude in the lives of those I encounter. Amen.

**Who is someone in your life that you're particularly grateful for, and how can
you express that gratitude to them today?**

Week 45. Cultivating Inner Peace

Day 309: FIND PEACE IN GOD'S PRESENCE

"You will keep in perfect peace those whose minds are steadfast, because they trust in you"
(Isaiah 26:3, NIV)

Heavenly Father, I come before You seeking the perfect peace that only You can provide. In a world full of chaos and uncertainty, I long for the steadfast assurance of Your presence. Help me to fix my mind on You, trusting in Your unfailing love and sovereign control over every aspect of my life.

Lord, when anxious thoughts threaten to overwhelm me, draw my focus back to You. Teach me to dwell in Your presence moment by moment, finding refuge in the shelter of Your wings. Help me to cultivate that trust more deeply each day. Amen.

**What practical step can you take today to fix your mind
on God and cultivate His peace in your daily life?**

Day 310: OVERCOME ANXIETY WITH PRAYER

*"Do not be anxious about anything, but in every situation, by prayer
and petition, with thanksgiving, present your requests to God."*
(Philippians 4:6, NIV)

Gracious God, I confess that anxiety often creeps into my heart, robbing me of peace and joy. Thank You for inviting me to bring every concern, no matter how big or small, to You in prayer. Help me to develop the habit of turning to You first when worries arise.

Father, teach me to pray with both honesty and thanksgiving, even in the midst of challenging circumstances. When anxious thoughts threaten to consume me, remind me of Your faithfulness in the past and Your promises for the future. Amen.

What specific anxiety can you surrender to God in prayer right now?

*"Peace I leave with you; my peace I give you. I do not give to you as the world gives.
Do not let your hearts be troubled and do not be afraid."
(John 14:27, NIV)*

Prince of Peace, I thank You for the precious gift of Your peace that You freely offer to me. Help me to fully embrace and experience this peace that surpasses all understanding. When the troubles of this world threaten to disturb my tranquility, remind me that Your peace is not dependent on my circumstances but on Your unchanging nature.

Lord Jesus, I choose to receive Your peace today. Guard my heart against fear and anxiety, replacing them with Your comforting presence. May Your peace be evident in my life, drawing others to the source of true comfort. Amen.

**How can you actively choose to embrace God's
peace in a specific situation you're facing today?**

Day 312: CULTIVATE A QUIET SPIRIT

*"A gentle answer turns away wrath, but a harsh word stirs up anger"
(Proverbs 15:1, NIV)*

Gentle Savior, I come to You asking for help in cultivating a quiet and gentle spirit. In a world that often values loudness and aggression, teach me the power of Your gentleness. Lord, tame my tongue and guard my heart, that my words may be a source of peace rather than conflict.

When I'm tempted to react harshly, remind me of the impact my words can have. Help me to be quick to listen, slow to speak, and slow to become angry. May the quietness of my spirit be a reflection of Your love and a testimony to Your transforming work in my life. Help me to follow in Your footsteps, bringing Your peace into every interaction. Amen.

**In what relationship or situation do you need to
practice responding with gentleness this week?**

"Come to me, all you who are weary and burdened, and I will give you rest"
(Matthew 11:28, NIV)

Compassionate Father, I come to You today weary and burdened, accepting Your invitation to find rest in Your presence. Thank You for understanding my exhaustion and for offering the perfect rest that only You can provide. Help me to release my burdens into Your capable hands, trusting in Your care and provision.

Lord Jesus, teach me what it means to truly rest in You. When I'm tempted to carry my burdens alone or seek rest in worldly distractions, draw me back to Your comforting embrace. Refresh my spirit, renew my mind, and restore my strength as I lean on You. Amen.

How can you practically set aside time to rest in His presence?

Day 314: TRUST IN GOD'S SOVEREIGNTY

"And we know that in all things God works for the good of those
who love him, who have been called according to his purpose"
(Romans 8:28, NIV)

Sovereign Lord, I come before You, acknowledging Your supreme authority over all things. Help me to trust in Your perfect plan, even when circumstances seem chaotic or painful. Increase my faith to believe that You are working all things together for my good and for Your glory.

Father, when I'm tempted to doubt Your goodness or question Your ways, remind me of Your unfailing love and wisdom. Give me the courage to surrender my own plans and desires to Your sovereign will. May my life be a testimony to Your faithfulness, inspiring others to trust in Your perfect timing and purposes. Help me to rest in the knowledge of Your sovereignty, finding peace in every situation as I trust in Your good and perfect plan. Amen.

Can you identify a situation where you need to trust God's sovereignty more fully? How can you surrender that to Him today?

"Bear with each other and forgive one another if any of you has a grievance against someone. Forgive as the Lord forgave you"
(Colossians 3:13, NIV)

Merciful God, I come to You grateful for the forgiveness You've so freely given me through Christ. Help me to extend that same forgiveness to others, even when it's difficult. Give me the strength to let go of grudges and the courage to initiate reconciliation where relationships have been broken.

Lord, when I'm tempted to hold onto bitterness or seek revenge, remind me of the immeasurable debt You've forgiven me. Soften my heart towards those who have wronged me and help me to see them through Your eyes of compassion. Amen.

What steps can you take to extend forgiveness to someone?

Week 46. Finding Strength in Trials

Day 316: PERSEVERE THROUGH HARDSHIPS

"Not only so, but we also glory in our sufferings, because we know that suffering produces perseverance"
(Romans 5:3, NIV)

Heavenly Father, I come before You, acknowledging the hardships and sufferings in my life. It's not easy to find glory in these difficult times, but I trust in Your word that these trials are producing perseverance in me. Grant me the strength to endure, knowing that You are shaping my character through these challenges.

Lord, when I feel overwhelmed by my circumstances, remind me of Your presence and Your purpose. Help me to see beyond my current struggles to the growth and strength that will result. May my perseverance through hardships be a testimony to Your sustaining grace. Amen.

What current hardship are you facing, and how can you persevere through it?

*"These have come so that the proven genuineness of your faith—o
f greater worth than gold, which perishes even though refined by fire—
may result in praise, glory and honor when Jesus Christ is revealed."*
(1 Peter 1:7, NIV)

Refining God, I acknowledge that the trials I face are part of Your process to purify and strengthen my faith. Help me to trust in Your wisdom and love, even when the refining fire feels intense.

Lord, when I'm tempted to question Your methods or resist the refining process, remind me of the preciousness of a tested faith. May I emerge from each trial with a faith that is stronger, purer, and more resilient. Thank You for valuing my faith even more than gold. Help me to cooperate with Your refining work in my life, looking forward to the day when it will result in praise, glory, and honor to You. Amen.

**How can you change your perspective on a current trial
to see it as part of God's refining process in your life?**

*"Even though I walk through the darkest valley, I will fear no evil,
for you are with me; your rod and your staff, they comfort me"*
(Psalm 23:4, NIV)

Loving Shepherd, as I navigate through the dark valleys of life, I cling to the promise of Your constant presence. Thank You for being with me in every circumstance, guiding and protecting me. May I feel the reassurance of Your nearness, especially in my darkest moments.

Let Your presence dispel my fears and fill me with courage to face whatever lies ahead. Thank You for being my faithful Shepherd, leading me through every valley, and bringing me safely to the other side. Help me to trust in Your guidance and find rest in Your comforting presence. Amen.

**In what specific situation do you need to be more
aware of God's comforting presence today?**

"But he said to me, 'My grace is sufficient for you, for my power is made perfect in weakness.' Therefore I will boast all the more gladly about my weaknesses, so that Christ's power may rest on me"
(2 Corinthians 12:9, NIV)

Almighty God, I come before You, acknowledging my weaknesses and limitations. Thank You for the promise that Your grace is sufficient and that Your power is made perfect in my weakness. Help me to embrace my frailties as opportunities for Your strength to shine through me.

Lord, when I'm tempted to hide my weaknesses or rely on my own strength, remind me that Your power is most evident when I am at my weakest. Help me to boast not in my own abilities, but in the amazing work You do through me despite my limitations. Amen.

What weakness or limitation can you surrender to God today?

Day 320: MAINTAIN HOPE IN TRIALS

"Not only so, but we also glory in our sufferings, because we know that suffering produces perseverance; perseverance, character; and character, hope"
(Romans 5:3-4, NIV)

Faithful God, I come to You seeking hope in the midst of my trials. Thank You for the promise that my sufferings are not meaningless, but are producing perseverance, character, and, ultimately, hope. Help me to maintain a perspective of hope, even when circumstances seem bleak.

Lord, when I'm tempted to despair or lose heart, remind me of the chain reaction of growth that You are initiating through my trials. May I see each challenge as an opportunity for You to develop my character and deepen my hope in You. Let the hope that springs from perseverance shine brightly in my life, encouraging others who may be struggling. Amen.

How can you actively cultivate hope in your current situation?

"Consider it pure joy, my brothers and sisters, whenever you face trials of many kinds, because you know that the testing of your faith produces perseverance"
(James 1:2-3, NIV)

Wise Father, I confess that it's often difficult to find joy in the face of trials. Yet I thank You for the growth and perseverance that come through challenges. Help me to see my trials through Your eyes, recognizing them as opportunities for spiritual maturity and deepened faith.

Give me the strength to persevere and the wisdom to learn the lessons You have for me in each trial. May my response to challenges be a testimony to Your grace and faithfulness. Thank You for the promise that You work all things, even trials, for my good and Your glory. Amen.

What specific lesson or growth opportunity can you identify in a current challenge you're facing?

Day 322: TRUST GOD'S FAITHFULNESS

"No temptation has overtaken you except what is common to mankind. And God is faithful; he will not let you be tempted beyond what you can bear. But when you are tempted, he will also provide a way out so that you can endure it"
(1 Corinthians 10:13, NIV)

Faithful God, I thank You for Your promise to be with me in every temptation and trial. Help me to trust in Your faithfulness, knowing that You will never allow me to face more than I can handle with Your help. Give me discernment to recognize the ways of escape You provide and the strength to choose them.

Lord, when I feel overwhelmed by temptations or trials, remind me that I am not alone in my struggles. May I find comfort in knowing that You understand my challenges and that You are always faithful to provide a way through them. Help me to grow in my trust in You. Amen.

What specific temptation are you facing right now?

Day 323: RECOGNIZE GOD AS THE GIVER

*"Every good and perfect gift is from above, coming down from the Father
of the heavenly lights, who does not change like shifting shadows"
(James 1:17, NIV)*

Heavenly Father, I come before You with a heart full of gratitude, recognizing that every blessing in my life comes from You. Thank You for Your constant generosity and love. Help me to see Your hand in both the big and small gifts that fill my days.

Lord, open my eyes to the many ways You provide for me and show Your love through Your gifts. May I never take Your blessings for granted but always approach You with a thankful heart. Help me to trust in Your goodness, even when I don't understand Your ways. Amen.

How can you express your gratitude for God's gifts today?

Day 324: APPRECIATE THE GIFT OF SALVATION

*"For it is by grace you have been saved, through faith—
and this is not from yourselves, it is the gift of God"
(Ephesians 2:8, NIV)*

Gracious Savior, I come before You overwhelmed by the magnitude of Your gift of salvation. Thank You for the undeserved grace that rescued me and gave me new life in Christ. Help me to never take this precious gift for granted but to live each day in gratitude for the salvation You've provided.

Lord Jesus, when I'm tempted to rely on my own efforts or merit, remind me that salvation is entirely Your gift, received through faith. May the reality of this gift transform how I live, motivating me to share Your love with others. Amen.

**How can you express your appreciation for
the gift of salvation in a tangible way today?**

"Children are a heritage from the Lord, offspring a reward from him"
(Psalm 127:3, NIV)

Loving Father, I thank You for the precious gift of family. Whether by blood or by choice, You have blessed me with people to love and who love me in return. Help me to cherish these relationships and to see them as the valuable heritage You intend them to be. Give me wisdom and patience in nurturing family bonds and grace in navigating family challenges.

Lord, when family life becomes difficult, or I'm tempted to take my loved ones for granted, remind me of the reward and responsibility that family represents. May I reflect Your love in my family relationships, offering forgiveness, support, and encouragement. Amen.

What is one specific way you can show appreciation for a family member today?

"A friend loves at all times, and a brother is born for a time of adversity"
(Proverbs 17:17, NIV)

Faithful God, thank You for friends who encourage me, challenge me, and point me towards You. Help me to be grateful for these relationships and to nurture them with care and intentionality. Give me wisdom to be the kind of friend that reflects Your love and faithfulness.

Lord, when I face adversity, remind me of the support system You've provided through my friends. May I also be ready to stand by others in their times of need. Help me to be a source of Your love and grace in my friendships, valuing these relationships as the precious gifts they are. In Jesus' name, Amen.

Who is a friend you're particularly thankful for? How can you express your appreciation to them and be a better friend in return?

"But he gives us more grace. That is why Scripture says:
'God opposes the proud but shows favor to the humble'"
(James 4:6, NIV)

Merciful Father, I come before You in awe of Your abundant grace. Thank You for continually pouring out Your favor upon me, even when I fall short. Help me to fully embrace and appreciate this unmerited gift, recognizing my constant need for Your grace in every aspect of my life.

Lord, when pride creeps into my heart, remind me of my dependence on Your grace. Teach me to walk in humility, always acknowledging that any good in me is a result of Your gracious work. May Your grace transform me from the inside out, enabling me to extend that same grace to others. Help me to live in the freedom and power of Your grace, reflecting Your love and mercy to the world around me. Amen.

In what area of your life do you most need to embrace God's grace today?

Day 328: APPRECIATE THE GIFT OF CREATION

"The heavens declare the glory of God; the skies proclaim the work of his hands"
(Psalm 19:1, NIV)

Creator God, I stand in awe of the beauty and complexity of Your creation. Thank You for the gift of this magnificent world that declares Your glory and proclaims Your handiwork. Help me to see Your creativity and power in the world around me, from the vastness of the skies to the intricacy of the smallest flower.

Lord, when I'm rushed or distracted, remind me to pause and appreciate the wonders of Your creation. May the beauty of nature draw my heart to worship You and inspire me to be a good steward of the earth. Let my appreciation for Your creation lead me to a deeper love and reverence for You, the Master Artist. Amen.

How does God's creation around you reflect God's character to you?

*"Each of you should use whatever gift you have received to serve others,
as faithful stewards of God's grace in its various forms."
(1 Peter 4:10, NIV)*

Generous God, I thank You for the spiritual gifts You've bestowed upon me and upon all believers. Help me to recognize, appreciate, and develop the unique gifts You've given me. Give me wisdom to use these gifts not for my own glory, but to serve others and build up the body of Christ.

Lord, when I'm tempted to compare my gifts to others or to doubt their value, remind me that each gift is a manifestation of Your grace. Help me to encourage others in the use of their gifts and to work in harmony with my brothers and sisters in Christ. Let my use of spiritual gifts be a testimony to Your grace and love at work in the world. Amen.

**What spiritual gift has God given you that
you can use to serve others this week?**

Week 48. Being a Living Testimony

Day 330: SHINE GOD'S LIGHT

*"In the same way, let your light shine before others, that they
may see your good deeds and glorify your Father in heaven"
(Matthew 5:16, NIV)*

Heavenly Father, I thank You for the light of Your love that shines in my heart. Help me to be a beacon of Your light in this world, reflecting Your goodness and grace through my words and actions. Give me the courage to shine brightly, even in dark or challenging situations.

Lord, when I'm tempted to hide my faith or blend in with the crowd, remind me of my calling to be Your light-bearer. Let Your light shine through me in such a way that others are drawn to Your love and truth. Help me to shine Your light consistently and authentically in every area of my life. Amen.

**What specific "good deed" can you do today that will shine
God's light and potentially draw others to Him?**

"Whatever happens, conduct yourselves in a manner worthy of the gospel of Christ"
(Philippians 1:27, NIV)

Righteous God, I come before You, asking for strength and wisdom to live a life of integrity. Thank You for the example of Christ and the guidance of Your Word. Help me to conduct myself in a manner that honors You and reflects the truth of the gospel. Give me the courage to stand firm in my convictions, even when it's difficult or unpopular.

Lord, when I'm faced with temptations or ethical dilemmas, remind me of the high calling I have in Christ. May my actions align with my beliefs, demonstrating the transforming power of the gospel in my life. Let my integrity be a testimony to Your faithfulness and grace. Help me to live in a way that brings glory to Your name and draws others to the truth of the gospel. Amen.

What specific step can you take today to
better align your actions with your faith?

Day 332: SHARE YOUR FAITH

"But in your hearts revere Christ as Lord. Always be prepared to
give an answer to everyone who asks you to give the reason for the
hope that you have. But do this with gentleness and respect"
(1 Peter 3:15, NIV)

Lord Jesus, I acknowledge You as the Lord of my life and the source of my hope. Give me the wisdom and courage to share my faith with others. Help me to be always prepared to give an answer for the hope I have in You, doing so with gentleness and respect.

Holy Spirit, guide my words and actions so that they create opportunities to share my faith. When those opportunities arise, fill me with Your wisdom and love. Help me to overcome any fear or hesitation in sharing my faith, trusting that You will use my words for Your glory. Amen.

Who is someone in your life that you can share your faith with this week?

"By this, everyone will know that you are my disciples, if you love one another"
(John 13:35, NIV)

Loving Father, I thank You for the perfect example of love demonstrated through Your Son, Jesus Christ. Help me to reflect that same selfless, sacrificial love in my relationships with others. May my love for fellow believers be a powerful testimony to the world of Your transforming grace.

Lord Jesus, give me the strength to love even those who are difficult to love, just as You have loved me unconditionally. Let my love for others be genuine, patient, and enduring. Help me to contribute to a culture of love within Your church that draws others to You and brings glory to Your name. Amen.

**How can you demonstrate Christ's love in a
tangible way to someone in your life today?**

Day 334: SERVE OTHERS SELFLESSLY

*"For even the Son of Man did not come to be served,
but to serve, and to give his life as a ransom for many"*
(Mark 10:45, NIV)

Servant King, I am humbled by Your example of selfless service. Thank You for showing us the true meaning of greatness through Your sacrificial love. Help me to follow in Your footsteps, serving others with a humble and generous heart. Give me eyes to see the needs around me and the willingness to meet them.

Lord Jesus, when I'm tempted to seek my own comfort or recognition, remind me of Your servanthood. May my life be characterized by putting others first and serving without expectation of return. Let my service be a reflection of Your love and a testimony to Your grace. Thank You for the opportunities You provide to serve others in Your name. Amen.

**What is one way you can selflessly serve someone
today, following Christ's example?**

"Bear with each other and forgive one another if any of you
has a grievance against someone. Forgive as the Lord forgave you"
(Colossians 3:13, NIV)

Merciful God, I thank You for the incredible forgiveness You've extended to me through Christ. Help me to extend that same forgiveness to others, even when it's difficult. Give me the strength to let go of grudges and the courage to initiate reconciliation where relationships have been broken.

Lord, when I'm tempted to hold onto bitterness or seek revenge, remind me of the immeasurable debt You've forgiven me. Soften my heart towards those who have wronged me and help me to see them through Your eyes of compassion. Help me to continually choose forgiveness, just as You continually forgive me. Amen.

Is there someone you need to forgive? What step can you take today towards extending that forgiveness and seeking reconciliation?

Day 336: PERSEVERE IN FAITH

"I have fought the good fight,
I have finished the race, I have kept the faith"
(2 Timothy 4:7, NIV)

Faithful God, I thank You for sustaining me in my journey of faith. I also thank You for the cloud of witnesses who have gone before me, showing that it's possible to finish well. Lord, while I'm here on Earth, give me the strength and determination to persevere, even when the path is difficult. Help me to fight the good fight, to run the race with endurance, and to keep the faith until the very end.

Lord Jesus, when I face trials or become weary, remind me of Your faithfulness and the eternal reward that awaits. May my perseverance in faith be an encouragement to others and a testimony to Your sustaining grace. Amen.

What challenges to your faith are you currently facing?

Day 337: SEEK GOD WHOLEHEARTEDLY

"You will seek me and find me when you seek me with all your heart"
(Jeremiah 29:13, NIV)

Heavenly Father, I come before You with a desire to seek You wholeheartedly. Thank You for Your promise that when I seek You with all my heart, I will find You. It's amazing to think that You are not hiding from me, but are eagerly waiting for me to seek You. Help me to seek You not just in times of need, but in every moment of every day.

Ignite in me a passionate pursuit of Your presence and truth. Remove any distractions or half-heartedness that keep me from fully seeking You. Lord, when I'm tempted to seek fulfillment in other things, remind me that true satisfaction is found only in You. Amen.

**What practical step can you take today to seek
God more wholeheartedly in your daily life?**

Day 338: ABIDE IN CHRIST

"Remain in me, as I also remain in you. No branch can bear fruit by itself; it must remain in the vine. Neither can you bear fruit unless you remain in me"
(John 15:4, NIV)

Lord Jesus, I thank You for the invitation to abide in You. Help me to remain deeply connected to You, drawing my strength, purpose, and identity from our relationship. Teach me what it means to truly abide in You day by day, moment by moment. May my life bear much fruit as I remain in close communion with You.

Savior, when I'm tempted to rely on my own strength or to disconnect from You in busyness, remind me that apart from You, I can do nothing of eternal value. Let my abiding relationship with You be evident through the love, joy, and peace that flow from my life. Amen.

How can you intentionally "abide in Christ" today?

"My sheep listen to my voice; I know them, and they follow me."
(John 10:27, NIV)

Good Shepherd, I thank You for speaking to me and for the privilege of hearing Your voice. Thank You for knowing me intimately and for the assurance that I can follow You with confidence. Help me to listen not just with my ears, but with my heart. Tune my ears to recognize Your voice amidst the noise of this world. Give me a heart that is eager to listen and quick to respond to Your guidance.

Lord Jesus, when I'm overwhelmed by other voices or my own thoughts, help me to quiet my heart and listen for Your still, small voice. May I grow in my ability to discern Your leading in my life. Let my obedience to Your voice be swift and complete, trusting that Your way is always best. Amen.

How can you create more space in your day to hear from Him?

Day 340: DELIGHT IN GOD'S PRESENCE

"You make known to me the path of life; you will fill me with joy
in your presence, with eternal pleasures at your right hand"
(Psalm 16:11, NIV)

Joyful God, I come before You with gratitude for the delight found in Your presence. Thank You for the promise of fullness of joy and eternal pleasures in Your company. Help me to find my greatest satisfaction and pleasure in spending time with You.

Lord, when I'm tempted to seek joy in lesser things, remind me of the unmatched delight of Your presence. May my time with You be characterized by joy, wonder, and adoration. Let the joy I find in Your presence overflow into every aspect of my life, drawing others to seek You. Amen.

What distractions or competing pleasures might you need to set aside?

"He has shown you, O mortal, what is good. And what does the Lord require of you?
To act justly and to love mercy and to walk humbly with your God"
(Micah 6:8, NIV)

Sovereign God, I come before You, acknowledging my need for a humble heart. Thank You for clearly showing me what is good and what You require. Help me to act justly, to love mercy, and above all, to walk humbly with You. Root out any pride or self-sufficiency in my heart.

Lord, when I'm tempted to exalt myself or to forget my dependence on You, remind me of my true position as Your servant and child. May my life be characterized by humble obedience to Your will. Let my humility before You translate into gracious interactions with others. Thank You for the example of humility set by Jesus. Amen.

How can you practice walking humbly with God today?

Day 342: PRIORITIZE TIME WITH GOD

"But seek first his kingdom and his righteousness,
and all these things will be given to you as well"
(Matthew 6:33, NIV)

Heavenly Father, I thank You for the invitation to seek Your kingdom and righteousness above all else. Help me to prioritize my relationship with You, putting time with You at the top of my daily agenda. Give me the wisdom to order my days in a way that reflects Your primacy in my life.

Lord Jesus, when the busyness of life threatens to crowd out my time with You, remind me of the importance of seeking You first. Thank You for the promise that as I seek Your kingdom first, You will provide for all my needs. Help me to trust in Your provision and to find my greatest fulfillment in pursuing You. Amen.

**What practical changes can you make to your
daily routine to prioritize time with God?**

"I keep asking that the God of our Lord Jesus Christ, the glorious Father, may give you the Spirit of wisdom and revelation, so that you may know him better"
(Ephesians 1:17, NIV)

Glorious Father, thank You for the privilege of knowing You personally. Today, I echo Paul's prayer, asking for Your Spirit of wisdom and revelation to know You better. Deepen my understanding of Your character, Your ways, and Your love.

Lord, when I'm tempted to be content with surface-level knowledge of You, stir in me a hunger for deeper revelation. May my life be characterized by an ever-increasing knowledge of You that transforms me from the inside out. Fuel my desire to grow in intimacy with You through Your Word and through prayer. Amen.

**How can you move beyond head knowledge to
heart knowledge in your relationship with Him?**

Week 50. Praying for Renewal and Restoration

Day 344: SEEK SPIRITUAL REVIVAL

"Will you not revive us again, that your people may rejoice in you?"
(Psalm 85:6, NIV)

God, I come to You today asking for spiritual revival. I feel the need for a fresh outpouring of Your Spirit in my life and in our community. Revive our hearts, Lord, and rekindle the flame of passion for You that may have dimmed over time.

Father, I pray for a renewed sense of Your presence and power in our midst. Shake us out of complacency and routine. Open our eyes to see You working in new and exciting ways. Let Your people rejoice in You once again. In Jesus' name, Amen.

**How can you actively seek and participate in spiritual
revival in your personal life and community?**

"He heals the brokenhearted and binds up their wounds."
(Psalm 147:3, NIV)

Heavenly Father, I come before You with my brokenness and wounds, both seen and unseen. I ask for Your healing touch in every area of my life that needs restoration. Thank You that You are the God who heals the brokenhearted and binds up our wounds.

Lord, I surrender to You the pain, disappointments, and hurts that I've been carrying. I ask for Your healing balm to soothe these wounded areas of my heart and life. May Your healing work in my life be a testimony to Your goodness and power. In Jesus' name, Amen.

What areas of your life need God's healing touch,
and how can you open yourself to receive His healing?

Day 346: PRAY FOR RENEWED STRENGTH

"But those who hope in the Lord will renew their strength. They will soar on wings like eagles; they will run and not grow weary, they will walk and not be faint"
(Isaiah 40:31, NIV)

Lord, I come to You feeling weary and in need of renewed strength. I place my hope fully in You, trusting in Your promise to renew the strength of those who wait on You. Fill me with Your divine energy and power to face the challenges before me.

Father, when I feel like I can't go on, lift me up on wings like eagles. Give me the endurance to run the race You've set before me without growing weary. When the path is long and difficult, grant me the persistence to keep walking without fainting. Renew my physical, emotional, and spiritual strength. In Jesus' name, Amen.

In what specific ways do you need God to renew your strength today?

"Create in me a pure heart, O God, and renew a steadfast spirit within me"
(Psalm 51:10, NIV)

Holy God, I come before You asking for a clean heart. Wash away any impurity, selfishness, or sin that has taken root in my heart. Create in me a pure heart that beats in rhythm with Yours, desiring what You desire and loving what You love.

Lord, along with a clean heart, I ask for a renewed and steadfast spirit. Strengthen my resolve to follow You faithfully. As You purify my heart and renew my spirit, use me as a vessel of Your love and grace in this world. May the purity of heart and steadfastness of spirit You create in me be evident in my words, actions, and attitudes. In Jesus' name, Amen.

What impurities or negative attitudes in your heart do you need to ask God to cleanse?

Day 348: SEEK RESTORATION OF JOY

"Restore to me the joy of your salvation and grant me a willing spirit, to sustain me"
(Psalm 51:12, NIV)

Joyful God, I come to You seeking a restoration of the joy of Your salvation. Reignite in me the wonder and excitement of knowing You and being known by You. Where circumstances or sin have dimmed my joy, I ask for a fresh outpouring of Your joy-giving Spirit.

Lord, along with restored joy, I ask for a willing spirit to sustain me. Make me eager to follow Your ways and quick to obey Your voice. When I face challenges or temptations, let this willing spirit strengthen my resolve to remain faithful to You. Father, as You restore my joy and grant me a willing spirit, use me to spread Your joy to others. In Jesus' name, Amen.

How can you cultivate and express the joy of your salvation in your daily life?

"Do not conform to the pattern of this world,
but be transformed by the renewing of your mind"
(Romans 12:2, NIV)

Transforming God, I come to You asking for a renewed mind. Help me to resist conforming to the patterns and thinking of this world. Instead, transform me by the renewing of my mind through Your Word and Your Spirit. Lord, align my thoughts with Your truth. Help me to recognize and reject lies and deceptions that creep into my thinking.

Fill my mind with thoughts that are true, noble, right, pure, lovely, admirable, excellent, and praiseworthy. Let my renewed mind lead to actions that reflect Your character and bring glory to Your name. In Jesus' name, Amen.

What worldly thought patterns do you need to replace with God's truth?

Day 350: TRUST GOD'S RESTORATIVE POWER

"And the God of all grace, who called you to his eternal glory in Christ, after you have
suffered a little while, will himself restore you and make you strong, firm and steadfast"
(1 Peter 5:10, NIV)

Gracious God, I thank You for Your promise to restore me and make me strong, firm, and steadfast. In times of suffering or difficulty, help me to trust in Your restorative power. I believe that You are working to bring beauty from ashes and strength from weakness.

Lord, I surrender to Your restoring work in my life. Even when I can't see or understand what You're doing, help me to trust that You are faithfully working all things for my good and Your glory. Strengthen my faith during times of waiting and uncertainty. May my journey of being restored and strengthened by You inspire hope in those who are suffering. Amen.

How has God restored you in the past, and how can you trust
Him for restoration in your current challenges?

Day 351: SEEK GOD'S GUIDANCE

*"Trust in the Lord with all your heart and lean not on your own understanding;
in all your ways submit to him, and he will make your paths straight"*
(Proverbs 3:5-6, NIV)

Heavenly Father, as I stand at the threshold of a new year, I seek Your guidance for the path ahead. Help me to trust You completely, setting aside my own limited understanding. I submit all my ways to You, knowing that You will direct my steps.

Lord, when I'm tempted to rely on my own wisdom or the world's advice, remind me to turn to You first. Give me the courage to follow Your leading, even when it doesn't make sense to me. Let my straight paths be a testimony to Your faithfulness and wisdom. In Jesus' name, Amen.

How can you actively seek God's guidance as you plan for the new year?

Day 352: SET GODLY GOALS

"Commit to the Lord whatever you do, and he will establish your plans"
(Proverbs 16:3, NIV)

Lord, as I set goals for the coming year, I commit them all to You. Guide me in establishing plans that align with Your will and bring glory to Your name. Help me to seek Your kingdom first in all my aspirations. Give me wisdom to discern between my desires and Your plans for me. When my goals seem overwhelming or impossible, remind me that with You, all things are possible.

Holy Spirit, as I work towards these goals, keep me dependent on You. May the process of setting and pursuing godly goals draw me closer to You and make me more like Christ. Let my commitment to You be evident in all I do. In Jesus' name, Amen.

What godly goals is God placing on your heart for the new year?

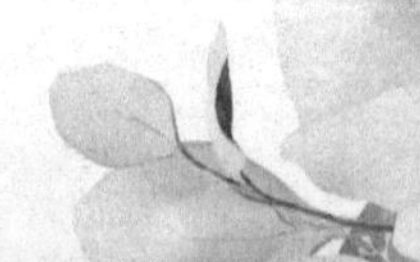

*"See, I am doing a new thing! Now it springs up; do you not perceive it?
I am making a way in the wilderness and streams in the wasteland."
(Isaiah 43:19, NIV)*

Creator God, I thank You for the gift of new beginnings. As I enter this new year, help me to perceive the new things You are doing in my life. Give me eyes to see the ways You are making in the wilderness and the streams You are creating in the wasteland.

Lord, when I'm tempted to cling to the familiar or fear change, remind me of Your power to make all things new. Grant me the courage to step into the new paths You are creating, trusting in Your guidance and provision. Father, use my journey to encourage others who may be stuck or afraid of change. In Jesus' name, Amen.

What new beginning is God inviting you to embrace in the coming year?

Day 354: TRUST GOD'S TIMING

*"There is a time for everything, and a season for every activity under the heavens"
(Ecclesiastes 3:1, NIV)*

Eternal God, as I look to the year ahead, help me to trust in Your perfect timing. Give me the patience to wait for the seasons You have ordained and wisdom to recognize when it's time to act. Align my heart with Your divine schedule.

Lord, when I'm tempted to rush ahead or lag behind, gently correct my pace. Help me to be content in every season, knowing that You are working out Your purposes in and through me. Grant me faith to trust Your timing, even when it differs from my own expectations. Use my journey to encourage others to find peace in Your perfect timing. In Jesus' name, Amen.

**In what area of your life do you need to trust
God's timing more fully in the coming year?**

"For I know the plans I have for you," declares the Lord, "plans to prosper you and not to harm you, plans to give you hope and a future."
(Jeremiah 29:11, NIV)

Loving Father, I thank You for Your promise of a hopeful future. As I look to the new year, fill me with hope and expectation for the good plans You have for me. Help me to trust in Your love and wisdom, even when circumstances seem uncertain. Lord, when doubts or fears about the future arise, remind me of Your faithful promises.

Give me the courage to hope boldly, grounded in the assurance of Your good intentions for my life. May my hope be a steady anchor for my soul in the year to come. Let my confident expectation in Your good plans be a source of encouragement to those who are struggling to see a positive future. In Jesus' name, Amen.

How can you actively cultivate and share hope for the future in the coming year?

Day 356: EMBRACE GOD'S CALLING

"For we are God's handiwork, created in Christ Jesus to do good works, which God prepared in advance for us to do"
(Ephesians 2:10, NIV)

Heavenly Father, I thank You for creating me with purpose. As I enter this new year, help me to fully embrace the calling You have placed on my life. Give me clarity to recognize the good works You have prepared for me to do. Day after day, remind me that I am Your handiwork, carefully crafted for Your purposes.

Grant me courage to step out in faith and fulfill the calling You have given me. May I find joy and fulfillment in doing the work You have prepared for me. Holy Spirit, guide me in discerning and pursuing God's calling in my life. In Jesus' name, Amen.

What steps can you take to more fully embrace and live out God's calling on your life in the new year?

"But grow in the grace and knowledge of our Lord and Savior Jesus Christ.
To him be glory both now and forever! Amen"
(2 Peter 3:18, NIV)

Gracious God, as I approach the new year, I ask for a deepening of my spiritual life. Help me to grow in Your grace and in the knowledge of Jesus Christ. Increase my hunger for Your Word and my desire for intimate fellowship with You.

Lord, show me areas where I need to mature spiritually. Give me discipline to cultivate holy habits that will nurture my growth. When I face challenges or setbacks, help me to see them as opportunities for spiritual development. Father, as I grow in grace and knowledge, may my life bring greater glory to You. In Jesus' name, Amen.

What specific area of spiritual growth do
you want to focus on in the coming year?

Week 52. Cultivating a Legacy of Faith

Day 358: PASS ON YOUR FAITH

"We will tell the next generation the praiseworthy deeds of the Lord,
his power, and the wonders he has done"
(Psalm 78:4, NIV)

Heavenly Father, thank You for the faith You've nurtured in me. Help me to pass on this precious gift to the next generation. Give me wisdom and opportunities to share Your praiseworthy deeds, power, and wonders with those who come after me.

Lord, when I feel inadequate or unsure about sharing my faith, remind me of the stories of Your faithfulness in my life. Grant me courage and clarity to communicate these truths effectively. May my words and actions consistently point others to You. Let the faith I pass on take root deeply and bear fruit abundantly. In Jesus' name, Amen.

How can you intentionally pass on your faith to the next generation today?

*"The integrity of the upright guides them,
but the unfaithful are destroyed by their duplicity"*
(Proverbs 11:3, NIV)

Righteous God, I pray for the strength to live a life of integrity that honors You. Guide me in being upright in all my ways, aligning my actions with my beliefs. Help me to be consistent in my character, whether in public or private.

Lord, when I'm tempted to compromise my integrity for personal gain or to avoid difficulty, remind me of the value You place on honesty and uprightness. Give me the courage to stand firm in my convictions, even when it's costly. Father, as I strive to live with integrity, use my example to inspire others to pursue righteousness. In Jesus' name, Amen.

In what area of your life do you need to cultivate greater integrity?

Day 360: LEAVE A GODLY EXAMPLE

*"Don't let anyone look down on you because you are young, but set an example
for the believers in speech, in conduct, in love, in faith and in purity"*
(1 Timothy 4:12, NIV)

Lord Jesus, help me to set a godly example in every area of my life. May my speech be gracious and uplifting, my conduct honorable, my love sincere, my faith unwavering, and my life pure. Use me as a living testimony of Your transforming power.

When I'm tempted to conform to the world's standards, remind me of my calling to be a godly example. Give me the strength to live in a way that inspires others to follow Christ. Help me to be mindful of the impact my life has on those around me. Holy Spirit, empower me to be a positive influence in my sphere of influence. As I strive to leave a godly example, may others be drawn to the light of Christ shining through me. Amen.

**How can you be more intentional about
setting a godly example in your daily life?**

*"And the things you have heard me say in the presence of many witnesses
entrust to reliable people who will also be qualified to teach others"*
(2 Timothy 2:2, NIV)

Heavenly Father, thank You for those who have invested in my spiritual growth. Without those people who had cared for my Spiritual life, I would not be here praying to You today. Help me to pay it forward by investing in others. Give me wisdom to identify reliable people I can entrust with the truths You've taught me.

Lord, guide me in mentoring and discipling others effectively. Grant me patience, love, and discernment as I share Your Word and my experiences with them. Help me to be a faithful steward of the knowledge and wisdom You've given me. Please use my efforts to create a ripple effect of spiritual growth and maturity. In Jesus' name, Amen.

Who is God calling you to invest in spiritually, and how can you start today?

Day 362: PERSEVERE IN FAITH

"I have fought the good fight, I have finished the race, I have kept the faith"
(2 Timothy 4:7, NIV)

Lord Jesus, You know how easily I get distracted from my walk with You. Give me the strength to persevere in my faith journey. Help me to fight the good fight, to run the race with endurance, and to keep the faith until the very end. When I face obstacles or grow weary, renew my determination to press on.

Father, when I'm tempted to give up or compromise my faith, remind me of the eternal significance of finishing well. Grant me the courage to face challenges head-on and the wisdom to navigate difficulties while staying true to You. Holy Spirit, empower me to leave a legacy of unwavering faith. In Jesus' name, Amen.

What area of your faith journey requires perseverance right now?

"Because of the Lord's great love we are not consumed, for his compassions never fail. They are new every morning; great is your faithfulness"
(Lamentations 3:22-23, NIV)

Faithful God, I pause to reflect on Your unwavering faithfulness in my life. Thank You for Your great love that sustains me and Your compassions that never fail. Help me to see and appreciate the new mercies You provide each morning.

Lord, when I'm tempted to doubt or forget Your faithfulness, bring to mind the countless ways You've proven trustworthy. Deepen my trust in You as I remember Your consistent care and provision throughout my life. Father, as I reflect on Your faithfulness, use my testimony to encourage others who may be struggling to see Your hand at work. In Jesus' name, Amen.

How has God demonstrated His faithfulness in your life this past year?

Day 364: RENEW YOUR COMMITMENT TO GOD

"But if serving the Lord seems undesirable to you, then choose for yourselves this day whom you will serve... But as for me and my household, we will serve the Lord"
(Joshua 24:15, NIV)

Sovereign Lord, I come before You today to renew my commitment to serve You. I choose once again to follow You wholeheartedly, submitting every area of my life to Your Lordship. Strengthen my resolve to honor You in all I do. Father, when the world offers competing allegiances, help me to stand firm in my decision to serve You alone. Give me the courage to live out this commitment daily, even when it's challenging or unpopular.

Holy Spirit, empower me to lead my household in serving the Lord. May my renewed commitment inspire those around me to choose Your ways. In Jesus' name, Amen.

**In what specific way can you demonstrate your
renewed commitment to serve God today?**

"May the God of hope fill you with all joy and peace as you trust in him, so that you may overflow with hope by the power of the Holy Spirit."
(Romans 15:13, NIV)

God of Hope, as I stand at the threshold of a new year, my heart fills with thanksgiving because I have You, God of the universe, who truly loves me and takes care of me. I know that You are already in the future, and You will remain faithful. As I face the coming of the new year, I have peace within my heart because I know that You are keeping me safe in my hands.

Lord, when uncertainties about the future arise, anchor me in the hope I have in You. Replace any fears or anxieties with Your perfect peace. May my trust in You be the foundation for a hope that remains steadfast in all circumstances.

Father, as I embrace hope for the future, use me to spread this hope to others. Let the joy and peace I find in You overflow to those around me, drawing them to the source of true hope. In Jesus' name, Amen.

What specific area of your life do you need to entrust to God's care as you step into the new year with hope?